Edward C. Mead

Historic Homes of the South-West Mountains, Virginia

Edward C. Mead

Historic Homes of the South-West Mountains, Virginia

ISBN/EAN: 9783337317775

Printed in Europe, USA, Canada, Australia, Japan

Cover: Foto ©ninafisch / pixelio.de

More available books at **www.hansebooks.com**

HISTORIC HOMES
OF THE
SOUTH-WEST
MOUNTAINS
VIRGINIA

BY EDWARD C. MEAD

AUTHOR OF "THE GENEALOGICAL HISTORY OF
THE LEE FAMILY OF VIRGINIA AND MARYLAND"

WITH TWENTY-THREE ILLUSTRATIONS
AND A MAP

PHILADELPHIA & LONDON
J. B. LIPPINCOTT COMPANY
1899

IN MEMORY OF THE PAST AND ESTEEM FOR THE PRESENT OWNERS OF THESE HISTORIC HOMES, THIS WORK IS INSCRIBED BY THE AUTHOR

PREFACE

THE celebrated section of the South-West Mountains, Virginia, stands as pre-eminently among her sister sections as does the Old Dominion in the galaxy of stars in the Union as the birthplace of Presidents, governors, and statesmen, as well as the seat of a refined and hospitable people.

The list of those who have lived here is a long and honored one. Many names are of such national celebrity that it is felt that any account of those who bore them and of the homes which so reflected their personality will be of more than local interest.

My object has been to do for these historic homes what Bishop Meade has already done for the churches of Virginia,—to perpetuate the characteristics of these famous houses along the South-West Mountains, many of which are fast disappearing under the advance of modern architecture, giving a faithful picture of each as they once stood, as well as an anecdotal account and brief genealogy of their inhabitants, thus embalming the traditions of these noble Virginia families.

PREFACE

To the many who have aided in the collection of the facts and incidents here recorded the writer returns his sincere thanks, trusting that, in handing down these family traditions portraying the simple, pure life of their forefathers, it may stimulate others to emulate their beautiful character, and perpetuate those good " old Virginia" customs, when

"Gallant Mirth was wont to sport awhile,
And serene old Age looked on with approving smile."

"Broad Oak,"
   Near Keswick, Virginia,
November, 1898.

CONTENTS

	PAGE
INTRODUCTION—THE SOUTH-WEST MOUNTAINS	11
Their Traditions; their People.	
MONTICELLO—THE HOME OF THOMAS JEFFERSON	21
Now owned by Hon. Jefferson M. Levy, of New York.	
PANTOPS—ONE OF JEFFERSON'S FARMS	41
Now owned by Professor John R. Sampson.	
LEGO—ONE OF JEFFERSON'S FARMS	49
The Home of the Taylors.	
SHADWELL—THE BIRTHPLACE OF THOMAS JEFFERSON	55
SHADWELL THE SECOND	63
EDGEHILL—THE HOME OF THE RANDOLPHS	65
BELMONT—THE HOME OF THE EVERETTS	75
EAST BELMONT—THE HOME OF ISAAC LONG, ESQ.	89
SUNNY SIDE—THE SUMMER RESIDENCE OF J. B. PACE, ESQ.	99
FRUITLAND—THE RESIDENCE OF A. P. FOX, ESQ.	107
CISMONT—THE SUMMER HOME OF COLONEL H. W. FULLER	111
CLOVER FIELDS—THE OLD HOME OF THE MERIWETHERS	129
Now owned by Frank M. Randolph, Esq.	
CASTALIA—THE ESTATE OF MURRAY BOOCOCK, ESQ.	139
MUSIC HALL—HOME OF THE LATE CAPTAIN JAMES TERRELL	153
BELVOIR—THE HOME OF THE NELSONS	159
KINLOCH—THE HOME OF DR. TOM MERIWETHER	167
Now owned by Aylett Everett, Esq.	

CONTENTS

	PAGE
MERRIE MILL—THE COUNTRY-SEAT OF JOHN ARMSTRONG CHANLER, ESQ.	179
ROUGEMONT—THE HOME OF THE DICKINSONS	187
HOPEDALE—THE HOME OF THE BOYDENS	193
CASTLE HILL—THE HOME OF THE RIVESES	201
KESWICK—THE HOME OF THE PAGES	217
EDGEWORTH—THE HOME OF THE GORDONS	231
COBHAM PARK—THE RESIDENCE OF THE LATE WILLIAM C. RIVES, JR.	241
THE MACHUNK FARMS—THE CREEK; CAMPBELLS; MACHUNK	247
BROAD OAK—THE HOME OF EDWARD C. MEAD, ESQ.	255
KESWICK STATION—CHESAPEAKE AND OHIO RAILROAD	263
EVERETTSVILLE—NOW LA FOURCHE, THE HOME OF THE BOWCOCKS	267
GLENMORE—THE HOME OF THE MAGRUDERS	271

LIST OF ILLUSTRATIONS

	PAGE
CASTLE HILL	*Frontispiece*
MAP OF THE SOUTH-WEST MOUNTAINS	11
MONTICELLO	21
PANTOPS	41
LEGO	49
SHADWELL	55
EDGEHILL	65
BELMONT	75
SUNNY SIDE	99
CISMONT	111
THE OLD COLONIAL KITCHEN AT CISMONT	126
CLOVER FIELDS	129
THE FIRST CLOVER FIELDS MANSION	133
CASTALIA	139
HERD OF HEREFORDS AT CASTALIA FARM	151
KINLOCH	167
MERRIE MILL MANSION	179
THE OLD COLONIAL MERRIE MILL	180
THE BATHING-POOL AT MERRIE MILL	183
HOPEDALE	193
CASTLE HILL MANSION	204
KESWICK	217
COBHAM PARK	241
BROAD OAK	255

INTRODUCTION

THE SOUTH-WEST MOUNTAINS: THEIR TRADITIONS; THEIR PEOPLE

THERE extends through the centre of Albemarle County, Virginia, a bold range of picturesque hills, the first that may be deemed mountains, as approaching from the east; these have their rise in Orange County, and terminate on the borders of James River, ranging in a south-west and north-east course parallel to and distant from the Blue Ridge about twenty miles.

This range has been known from an early period as the "South-West Mountains," so called from the direction in which they point.

The early history of Albemarle County, dating from its formation in 1744, is one of peculiar interest. Even before that period its mountains, valleys, and rivers had been explored by a venturesome people, among whom were such pioneers as Peter Jefferson, Robert Walker, William Randolph, Nicholas Meriwether, and Robert Lewis, who, upon reaching the colony, turned their footsteps from the already thickly settled eastern counties and sought the region of the wild "Apalata Mountains" of the west, to which the Indians pointed them; when, however, they reached this first range of blue hills, towering in solemn grandeur above the surrounding plain, they were so struck with their beauty and fertility that here they rested, and forever since their descendants have held this favored spot of Virginia by right of the king's patent.

Beginning at Monticello, the home of Thomas Jefferson, where the waters of the Rivanna, or "Riveranna," as then called, break through the little chain of mountains on their way to the James, and at short distances of a mile or less apart, scattered along the spurs and ridges of these mountain slopes, or nestled in valleys beside shady springs and rivulets, were the first settlements made. For some time the South-West Mountains formed the western limit of the colony, but when its dark-red alluvial soil was found to be particularly adapted to the culture of the great staple, tobacco, and its salubrious climate so refreshing to the fever-stricken emigrants, these favored hills were eagerly sought, and the county was early settled by a most intelligent and industrious race of people, who were peculiarly different in dialect, traits of character, and social intercourse from the general class of early settlers in America.

The following graphic description by Governor James Barbour, of Orange County, as taken from the *Farmers' Register* of 1835, gives an accurate idea of this celebrated range:

"This unique region of the South-West Mountains stretches from the Rappahannock to the James River. I have heard, indeed, of claims to a continuance of this peculiar soil as reaching farther both to the north and south. I can only say, as far as my observation has extended, these claims are not sustained. Its length may, therefore, be given at one hundred and ten miles, its average breadth five miles, containing three hundred and twenty thousand acres; its latitude in 37°–38° north. Of this tract of land, one-half at least in its virgin state was very fertile, a fourth sufficiently so to yield a fair return to labor, the other fourth sterile and rocky, but covered with fine timber, particularly the chestnut, whose duration in rails may be fixed at sixty or seventy years.

"The advantages of this region are many, and some of them peculiar. It presents the singular fact that the mountain is fertile to the summit,— one thousand feet being the highest point (Peter's), —and much more so than the country at its base. It is more abundantly watered than any I have ever seen; springs of cool living water are to be found in every dell; and on my own estate I have a copious and lasting spring near the top of the mountain, at an elevation of six hundred feet at least. Its vegetation is fourteen to twenty days in advance of the level conterminous country, and still it is usually exempt from the late frosts, while the fruit in the level country is destroyed by them.

"Mr. Jefferson told us the frost of May 4, 1774, while destroying even the forest-trees at the summit and at the foot of the mountain, left a zone of considerable breadth midway the mountain, where even the fruit escaped. The elevations on its western side present the most beautiful sites for building, furnishing, as they do to a great extent, a prospect of the Blue Ridge, distant twenty-five miles, and the intermediate country between; above all, we may fairly claim that no spot on earth is more healthy. Let us, the inhabitants of the South-West Mountains, rejoice and be grateful that our benefits greatly preponderate over our ills. And so far as my testimony goes, resulting from actual observation of near one-third of the entire circumference of the earth, I feel no hesitation in declaring that I deem them the most desirable abode I have ever seen."

In the above account a slight error is made in the altitude of Peter's Mountain (named in honor of Peter Jefferson, the father of the President), which stands nearly at the north-east terminus of the range, and forms its highest point. In the recent survey of this region, made by the "United States Coast and Geodetic Survey," the altitude of this peak is placed at fifteen hundred feet above the sea-level, the average height of the various knobs along the range being one thousand feet, while the hills along its base dwindle down to five hundred feet or less. The late Captain George C. Dickinson, whose reputation as a civil engineer was very high, gives the altitude of Peter's Mountain as eighteen hundred and fifty feet, and the average elevation of the various residences along its base as four hundred and forty feet.

The topography of the range is quite peculiar.

SOUTH-WEST MOUNTAINS

Its many prominent peaks ascend in height from south-west to north-east, at which point they terminate suddenly, dwindling into mere hills. Between each of these peaks are low gaps, through which roadways were early made to the western side, some of which still exist. Each of these high points and low gaps received their name from those who first settled near them, thus perpetuating their family's name by these living monuments.

The farms, or rather plantations, of the first few settlers were large, being immense grants of wild land from the crown, the boundaries of which frequently extended into the adjacent counties, the entire range of the South-West Mountains being at one time held by but two or three settlers, —Robert Walker, Nicholas Meriwether, and Peter Jefferson. Soon, however, these immense tracts were divided and even subdivided into strips of one thousand acres each, extending from the summit of the range to the lowlands at its foot, thus forming a series of settlements along its entire length from Charlottesville to Gordonsville.

The dwellings of these first settlers were generally rude log cabins, which the generous forests made easy to erect. They consisted usually of two rooms, with a rough stone chimney between, perched beside some bold spring in the dense forest, which afforded the hardy frontiersmen comfort and security. Another generation, however, required a more portentous building, frequently made of rough boards, put on with hand-wrought nails. The style of many of these, some of which are still standing, partook usually of the Saxon or early Romanesque period of England; their distinguishing features being plainly seen in the high-peaked roof, wide fireplace, and immense buttress of its lofty chimney, so commonly seen during the last century. Again, in the course of time, these, too, would give place to a more modern structure, having two stories, a wide hall, and spacious rooms with large windows, or even be replaced by some stately brick edifice, thus effectually obliterating the old homestead of one hundred years ago, few of which stand to show under what contracted limits our forefathers lived.

But what of the people whose homes were nestled along the slopes of these beautiful foot-hills, upon which the first tinge of the rising sun lightens with its genial rays, spreading over them a halo of supreme peace and happiness? They were a plain, honest, straightforward class, struggling under the adversities of the age in which they lived, and wonderfully overcoming the difficulties which the Revolution placed upon them. They were open-hearted and generous to a fault, yet tenacious in their religious and political opinions; clannish to a degree, intermarrying for many generations, thus retaining their lands, their customs, and family traditions among themselves. But, alas! nearly all have passed away; they sleep in families of several generations in the little burying-lot attached to each home, and their once familiar family-seats have passed into the hands of strangers, who are fast removing the old landmarks, until, with very

SOUTH-WEST MOUNTAINS

few exceptions, none of these lands of a once proud people are now held by their descendants, from whom has passed forever a princely heritage under the original grant of a hundred years ago.

In tracing the history of these old homes and the peculiar traits of their first owners, we must not forget that they lived, as it were, in a primitive age and during the first formation of the country, even before many of the great inventions of this nineteenth century had materialized, or before the social revolution under which our country has recently passed. They lived most roughly in their log cabins, and under many difficulties,—lighting their fires with their flintlocks, moulding their pewter spoons and candles, as they did their bullets, in moulds brought with them from the old country, spinning, weaving, and making their own apparel, doing their daily work, or worshipping God on Sunday while holding the musket in one hand for fear of the treacherous Indian. And yet they were cheerful, hopeful, and courageous, with a love and pride for their new-found country which left no difficulty too great for their daring to maintain their sovereignty over it. This was Virginianism in the true sense of the word, which gained for their descendants this fair land, and the spirit in which it must always be maintained.

Though this peculiar people have retired behind the scenes, yet there come forward in their sons and daughters many noble representatives of the true Scotch-Irish stock, who as statesmen, lawyers, and men of science and letters are maintaining the splendid record of this noble old county for its eminent men. We are enabled in these pages to mention but few of her brilliant sons, and must leave her Minors, Dukes, Dabneys, Garths, Southalls, Woods, and a host of others who have won enviable fame, for another volume. In looking at these, we can truly exclaim there is no degeneracy, political, forensic, or scientific, for lamentation here; and as warriors they have proved worthy knights of the lance. It is war which sows the dragon's teeth that spring up in soldiers and heroes on every side, and our recent conflict has shown that the sons of the South have lost none of the valor of their veteran fathers.

Nor can we fail to mention the true Christian character of these old families of the South-West Mountains, who clung to their religion as the very lever of Archimedes, which, resting on another world, easily bears up all destinies of this; led as they were by that great father of the Episcopal Church in Virginia, Bishop Meade, who, in his "Old Churches and Families of Virginia," has left them a rich heritage; thus they could not fail to become eminent in church as well as in state, receiving continually, as they did, the blessings of a bountiful Providence.

In testimony of their firm faith, they have erected many beautiful and modest little Gothic houses of worship over these gentle slopes, surrounded by stately oaks, beneath whose umbrageous arms sleep some of those whose lives we have but slightly sketched.

SOUTH-WEST MOUNTAINS

Thus we have endeavored to adequately portray this noted range of mountains, where are seated the historic homes to be noted, but no language or pencil can give a perfect idea of their true beauty and impressive aspect, as when first seen in all their solemn grandeur. No wonder Mr. Jefferson called it the "garden spot of Virginia;" no wonder its first settlers were charmed by such a sight, where Nature seemed to have perfected herself for the happiness of man; no wonder it has been the theme of poets and philosophers from time immemorial. Nor is this celebrity confined to its beautiful scenery alone; here is the home of the richest fruits of the soil, especially of that superb apple the "Albemarle pippin," which has gained the recognition of the Queen of England; here are generous products of the mineral kingdom, such as granite and slates of varying colors; here the floral kingdom bestows her choicest hues; surely, few counties can present such a *menu* to entice the lover of nature. Yet, above all, here is that noble seat of learning, the University of Virginia, made famous by Jefferson himself, from which have emanated some of the most brilliant minds of the past century, whose records have become national; for as the rich soil along the South-West Mountains, upon which they lived, made them independent, they also grew to be intellectual giants, and became not only controllers of the soil, but also ruled the nation, rising in eminence with the State and Union, until all eyes were turned in wonder to this little region of

HISTORIC HOMES

Albemarle which had produced so many great men.

Nor can we more faithfully picture those who have lived at the foot of these towering hills than in the words of Wirt, who said that "the people of Albemarle were the society of nature;" and this most truthfully represents them, as, like the beauties of nature around them, they partook of the beautiful in character.

> "Search the land of living men,
> Where wilt thou find their like agen?"

MONTICELLO

MONTICELLO

THE HOME OF THOMAS JEFFERSON

NEXT to Mount Vernon, doubtless there is no place in the Union that has been more written of or more visited than Monticello, the beautiful home of President Jefferson; and yet of the many who have visited this historic spot, and the much that has been said of it, few are aware of the true story connected with the building of this celebrated mansion.

Many legends and marvellous tales are told the stranger who treads its portals, few of which are based upon fact; yet there remain many incidents untold which would add an interesting page to its history, which we propose to gather up and trace the true story of its erection, from its inception to its completion.

Colonel Peter Jefferson, the father of Thomas Jefferson, and William Randolph, both of Goochland County, Virginia, were very close friends and neighbors. In 1735 both obtained "patents" for large grants of land lying contiguous to each other, and ever since their descendants have intermarried and maintained this juxtaposition.

Colonel Peter Jefferson had thus obtained by grant one thousand acres, lying on each side of the Rivanna River, where it intersects the South-

West range of mountains; to this he added by purchase nine hundred acres, making a total of nineteen hundred acres of land on each side of the river, which embraced the little towns of Shadwell on the north and Milton on the south.

In 1770, Mr. Jefferson, who was then a young practising lawyer, first began to clear the summit of Monticello (Italian for "little mountain") with a view of building. It was then merely a wild, tangled forest, but he had often looked upon this elevated spot with peculiar attraction, and had frequently rambled over its steep, craggy sides, or clambered to its summit, there to gaze upon the grand panoramic view spread out before him with feelings of sublime admiration and intense delight; it was such a picture as he wished always before him, and thus it was he decided here to build his home.

After the destruction by fire of the paternal roof at Shadwell, Mr. Jefferson began in earnest to build upon this almost inaccessible spot, and in the fall of that year (1770) had erected a small one-and-a-half-story brick building, containing one good-sized room, which is the same portion of the present building forming the southeast "pavilion" at the extremity of the south "terrace;" this room was the only part of the house habitable when he took his young bride there in 1772.

Mr. Jefferson's conception and designs for building his new home were not so elaborate or extensive as were afterwards carried out upon his return from Europe. He was very conventional

SOUTH-WEST MOUNTAINS

in his style and manner of living, not wishing to go beyond the simplicity of his neighbors, even in his plan of building, and yet there was at that time not another brick building outside the town of Charlottesville, and, though of quite moderate proportions compared to its ultimate appearance, it was then considered the most imposing building in the county.

The belief that Mr. Jefferson imported from England most of the brick used for his building is quite erroneous; all these were made upon the spot by his slaves, and the site of their manufacture is still pointed out; but in after-years, when completing the north end and adding many embellishments to his original design, some of the finest brick and ornamental material were procured in Philadelphia and sent around by water to Richmond, and thence to the little town of Milton.

In the autumn of 1775 still further additions were made, and the grounds greatly improved and enlarged, Mr. Jefferson planting with his own hands many fruit and ornamental trees, the trunks of which still remain.

During the sessions of Congress, while Mr. Jefferson would be absent from Monticello for months at a time, the work of completion would be necessarily slow, and even up to the year 1782 the house was but partially completed. Still more did that part which had already been built suffer much from delay during his sojourn in France as ambassador. It was not until Mr. Jefferson's return in 1794 that real active work was resumed, and he applied himself enthusiastically once more to the early completion of his design.

Mr. Jefferson had not been very favorably impressed with foreign architecture, though this may be attributable to a little democratic pride for his own country. He thus writes:

"The city of London is handsomer than Paris, but not so handsome as Philadelphia. Their architecture is the most wretched style I ever saw, not meaning to except America, where it is bad, or even Virginia, where it is worse."

On March 10, 1793, he thus writes concerning the new addition:

"I have it much at heart to run up the part of the house the latter part of the summer and fall, which I had proposed to do in the spring."

He also makes mention this year,—

"The trees planted nearest the house at Monticello are not yet full grown," and he sighs for shade.

Again he says,—

"I have my house to build, my fields to farm and to watch, for the happiness of those who labor for mine,"—meaning his daughter Martha and her husband, Thomas Mann Randolph.

His intention now was to build another wing, one story and a half high, both to be united and crowned with a balustrade, having a dome between them, the apartments to be large and convenient, the decorations within and without to be simple, yet regular and elegant.

Mr. Jefferson had already erected a saw-mill, a grist-mill, and a nail-factory, where every nail for the building was hand-forged by his colored boys. Many of his artisans had been brought with him from Europe, and with all the material at hand the work now progressed rapidly.

The story that Mr. Jefferson labored upon the building and laid many of the brick with his own hand is also erroneous. He was always fond of working in his "shop," where in this "mechanical retreat," which stood at the rear of the house, he would put to a practical test his theories, constructing models of farm implements and exercising his inventive genius; but he never labored in the real sense of the word, except for his own gratification and pleasure, or to set an example of industry to those around him.

In the fall of 1795 more brick were burnt for the completion of his new design, and in March, 1796, he thus writes to a friend:

"I have begun the demolition of my house, and hope to get through its re-edification in the course of the summer. We shall have the eye of a brick-kiln to poke you into or an octagon to air you in."

In November, 1796, the new walls of the house were so far completed that but little more than a week was wanted to get them ready for roofing, when a sudden cold spell stopped all further work for that year; such was the cold that on the 23d of the month the ground was hard frozen and remained so all winter. In 1797 the new portion of the house had been roofed in and was nearly completed, but in the following year the house was again dismantled to renew the roof, and only the south pavilion, parlor, and study were fit for occupation.

In speaking of his many disasters, he sadly writes in 1798, as prophetic of the coming financial storm,—

"The unprofitable condition of Virginia estates in general leaves it now next to impossible for the holder of one to avoid ruin. If a debt is once contracted by a farmer, it is never paid but by a sale."

After having returned from Philadelphia in 1798 he continued to push the work on the house, in order to have all of his children with him; but in March, 1799, he writes,—

"Scarcely a stroke has been done to the house since I went away; so it has remained open at the north end another winter. It seems as if I should never get it habitable."

Even up to the year 1800 the building was in an unfinished state, and yet large numbers of guests would be entertained, besides having all his children around him. Though being somewhat incomplete outwardly, yet the internal work continued to progress during his term of the Presidency, the mansion then being occupied by his youngest daughter, Maria, and her husband, Mr. Eppes.

In June, 1801, the building met with another misfortune, caused by a severe hail-storm, which broke nearly every window-pane in the house, as well as the skylights on the roof, flooding the interior and driving the family out of doors. As it was extremely difficult to get glass in those days, we can readily imagine the pitiable situation in which the family was placed.

In 1802 the Monticello mansion was considered completed. The expense had been very great for those times, which, Mr. Jefferson states, was exactly two thousand and seventy-six dollars and twenty-nine cents, while he was away at Washington, besides the large sums he had previously expended upon it.

Thus it had taken nearly *thirty years* to build this historic old edifice, a building which could now be erected in six months under our present rapid mode of construction.

Let us glance for a moment at this curious structure as it then stood, fresh from the hands of the illustrious architect, for Mr. Jefferson had designed each part most minutely himself.

Entering from the eastern portico with its lofty Corinthian pillars and arched door, over which is still seen the old English clock which marked the hours, the visitor is here met and ushered through large, double glass doors into a spacious semi-octagonal hall with its wide fireplace at one end, as is usually found in old English mansions. Opposite the door is a small gallery, while on one side of it stood a fine marble bust of the patriot himself, and on the other one of Washington, both by the celebrated Italian artist Carracci. Along each side of the hall were many Indian relics which Mr. Jefferson had himself collected.

From this hall opens another glass door leading into the drawing-room or *salon*, being the largest and most handsome room in the house, and situated immediately under the dome. This room is also octagonal, its floor being laid in parquetry of octagonal blocks of different colored wood, which were cut and fitted by his own colored workmen, giving it a most unique and pleasing effect, and which for skill challenges the genius of a more intelligent race. The walls of this stately room were adorned with portraits of Columbus, Vespucius, Andrew Doria, Castruccio-Castracani, Raleigh, Cortez, Bacon, Newton, Locke, Washington, Adams, Madison, and Monroe, while on either side of the door stood the busts of Alexander and Napoleon.

Leading from this room on the west side was the dining-room, and beyond this the octagonal tea-room. Here were to be seen busts of Franklin, Voltaire, Lafayette, and Paul Jones. Adjoining this were the bedrooms for guests, while on the east of the entrance hall was the bedroom of Mrs. Martha Randolph, who resided there permanently after the death of Mrs. Jefferson.

Mr. Jefferson's bedroom was next to that of Mrs. Randolph, beyond which was his library, which extended to the west side of the house, and from which led into an arched conservatory; beyond this was Mr. Jefferson's celebrated workshop.

The upper part of the house was gained by a very narrow, tortuous stairway; the rooms above were quite small, of low pitch, and badly lighted or ventilated; all of them were of many shapes, in conformity to the octagonal design of the house; alcoves let into the wall served in the place of bedsteads, their small dimensions being hardly suited to the comfortable repose of an ordinary-sized person.

The dome over the parlor was covered with thick glass; this was called the "ladies' drawing-room," which at one time was used as a billiard-room until the laws of Virginia prohibited the game. It was also said to have been used as a "ballroom;" but it is safe to say that Mr. Jefferson never had a dancing party in his house, though extremely fond of music, and even had his daughters taught the graceful art.

The furniture throughout was very handsome, most of which was purchased in France, and used while living in Philadelphia. The beautiful marble and brazier tables, French mirrors, and elegant sofas of the court style of Louis XVI. gave a charming and effective contrast to the artistic finish of the interior; while the many rich paintings, statuary, and works of art gave a sense of regal splendor which amazed the many plain and simple Virginians who thronged the mansion.

Governor Gilmer, of Georgia, who was a frequent and familiar visitor, thus describes Monticello during Mr. Jefferson's last term of office:

"Three rooms of the house were left open for visitors. I saw statuary, fine paintings, and a collection of Indian relics. The statuary was very beautiful; I could not be satisfied with looking at it. The Indian remains were singular things. Mr. Jefferson's library door was locked, but the window-blinds were thrown back, so that I could see several books turned open upon the table, the inkstand, paper, and pens as they had been used when Mr. Jefferson quitted home."

He also thus describes the appearance of Mr. Jefferson in 1825, just previous to his death:

"He was still erect; his reddish hair slightly gray, his complexion florid, and his countenance intellectual. He described his plan for the university at Charlottesville, then under his particular direction, the great seat of learning for the Southern States. His advanced age and valuable public services, eminent abilities, social qualities, and controlling influence in organizing and giving directions to the Democratic party made him an object of special interest. It was, indeed, surprising to see one so old, who had been so industriously employed in discharging the most difficult public duties, so intent upon what he yet had to do."

But let us turn again to the building. On top of the dome Mr. Jefferson had his observatory, being a simple platform surrounded by a balustrade. Here he would often sit, night and day, surveying the heavens or the vast expanse of scenery before him with his telescope.

The famous nail-factory, machine-shops, and weaving-rooms were to the south-east of the house, beyond which was the terraced garden, in which he delighted to exhibit his horticultural products.

SOUTH-WEST MOUNTAINS

The farm itself had not been cleared to any great extent around the mansion, most of the crops being raised on the north side of the river at Shadwell and upon the Tufton farm near Milton,

Thus we find the farm and mansion of Monticello in 1809, upon the retirement of Mr. Jefferson from the Presidency. But it was not to gain repose, for he was followed to his beautiful mountain home by a host of admirers and visitors, and but for the records left us, it were scarcely possible to believe the extent to which the imposition upon his privacy by friends, kindred, and the public generally was carried at this time. They would come singly and in families, bringing babies, nurses, drivers, and horses, spending weeks and even months at a time, giving the place an appearance of some noted watering rendezvous. Here would be gathered students, savants, musicians, clergymen, members of Congress, foreign travellers, artists, and men of every faith and political creed to gratify their curiosity and say that they had seen and heard Mr. Jefferson. In one instance a family of six from Europe remained ten months; on another occasion a lady broke a pane of glass with her parasol in her eagerness to get a glimpse of the President. Crowds would stand about the house for hours watching for his exit, until Mr. Jefferson in desperation would fly to his farm, Poplar Forest, in Bedford County, for repose, expressing truly his feelings when he said, " Political honors are but splendid torments."

At various times there were also many celebrated

visitors to Monticello, who have left their record of the place as it then appeared; among these were the Duke de Laincourt, a distinguished French traveller, who, in 1796, remained several days; the Marquis de Chastellux, aide to General Lafayette; Lieutenant Hall, of the English army, in 1816; and William Wirt, the historian, the friend and frequent visitor of Jefferson. All these have given graphic descriptions of this celebrated spot, some in language most illusive, for it is hardly possible for the eye to reach the Chesapeake Bay, the Atlantic Ocean, or even to the James River, nor can the lofty hills of Maryland or the Peaks of Otter be seen, yet the view is grand, majestic, and inspiring, —the same which Mr. Jefferson gazed upon with delight, and which has been the theme of poets and historians since, and ever more to be the admiration of thousands who make their pilgrimage to this shrine of America's freedom.

Thus stood Monticello at the close of Mr. Jefferson's life in 1826. It was known at this time that he was deeply involved in debt,—one partially made in entertaining his numerous guests, —in consequence of which his entire estate was soon afterwards offered for sale by his grandson and executor, Colonel Thomas Jefferson Randolph, of Edgehill. Mr. Jefferson had truly rendered himself poor when he built Monticello. The Italians brought over to do the ornamental work proved most expensive, and his friends had literally "ate him out of house and home;" so of his once large estate of ten thousand acres very little remained besides the mansion and its contents, he having previously sold, in 1776, lands to the amount of twenty thousand dollars in the hope of stemming the incoming tide of insolvency.

About the year 1828, Commodore Uriah P. Levy, of the United States Navy, who had known and greatly admired Jefferson, secured the mansion with four hundred acres of the Monticello tract. In purchasing the place he designed to preserve it in the same condition, and carry out the plans of the great patriot himself for its adornment; and still further, in honor of his memory, he erected a handsome statue to him in the City Hall at New York.

Commodore Levy presided most gracefully over the halls of Monticello, and fittingly maintained its just celebrity for hospitality. As an instance of his extreme courtesy, it is stated that on one occasion, when a party of gentlemen visited the place, among whom was the Rev. Stephen Jackson, the father of the present Bishop Jackson, of Alabama, after showing them the house, the commodore opened a bottle of wine which he had brought direct from the island of Madeira; the Rev. Mr. Jackson, in drinking to the health of his host, said, "May you live long and prosper." Whereupon Commodore Levy replied, as he held up his glass, "And may your reverence bury me."

After the death of Commodore Levy the estate descended to his nephew, the Hon. Jefferson M. Levy, of New York, its present owner.

During the civil war it was confiscated by the Confederate government and fell into rapid decay;

at one time being used as a hospital, after which it was rented to unscrupulous parties, who allowed it to be sadly pillaged. After the war it was not difficult for Mr. Levy to regain possession, who at once began its restoration, and to-day it stands complete, and perhaps far more beautiful than even in Jefferson's time.

Let us picture Monticello as it now stands, after a lapse of nearly seventy years, still sitting in all its majestic pride and grandeur upon its lofty eminence, while so many of the great, the good, and the gifted who once graced its halls have passed away forever.

Instead of a steep, rough road, filled with rocks and gullies, upon which vehicles would once frequently stall, the visitor can now drive from the city of Charlottesville over a smooth and easily graded road, which winds gracefully around Carter's Mountain, bringing the traveller to the "Notch," or first summit, almost before he realizes it. Here stands a porter's lodge, with artistic double gate, through which vehicles enter upon the Monticello domain proper, and begin to ascend the Little Mountain, upon which the mansion sits a mile above. The same smooth road, bordered by a stone wall, winds along its rugged sides until the cemetery is reached, which stands midway to the summit.

This is the spot chosen by Jefferson, in 1782, after the death of his wife, Martha Wayles Jefferson, where he wished himself and family to be laid. It is on a gentle slope of the mountain, to the right of the road, surrounded by lofty oaks and pines, with all the solemn beauty and stillness of the primeval forest. Here he first laid his wife, and then his youngest daughter, Maria Eppes. Mr. Jefferson then had a rough stone wall four feet high placed around it, with a small iron gate for entrance. This was more as a protection from roaming cattle than from human depredation. These few graves were unmarked by any stone for several years, but after the death of Mr. Jefferson, in 1826, there was found in a private drawer, among other relics of his wife and daughter, a pen-and-ink sketch of a monument such as he wished to be placed over his own grave. It was to be eight feet high, of Virginia stone, with a suitable base, upon which was to be the following inscription:

"Here was Buried
THOMAS JEFFERSON,
Author of the Declaration of American Independence; of the Statutes of Virginia, for Religious Freedom, and Father of the University of Virginia.
Born April 2nd, 1743, O.S.
Died July 4th, 1826."

His wishes were scrupulously carried out by his grandson, Thomas Jefferson Randolph, and though the estate was burdened by heavy debts, yet the proffer by the Legislature of Virginia and other States to defray the expense was refused. There being no suitable stone in Virginia for the monument, it was ordered from the North, and cut from Vermont granite.

The inscription was cut upon a separate tablet of marble and let into the granite. This first monument was placed directly over the grave of Jefferson, which was five or six feet from, and directly opposite to, the entrance, the inscription facing the gate towards the east. Mrs. Jefferson lies on the right side of this monument. Soon after the death of his eldest daughter, Martha Wayles Randolph, in 1836, and her husband, Governor Thomas Mann Randolph, in 1828, both of whom are buried there, a higher and more substantial wall of brick was placed entirely around the old one, with a larger and stronger gate, to prevent the destruction of the monument by relic-seekers, which had already begun.

About the year 1875 the Senators from Virginia, led by the Hon. S. S. Cox, of New York, who had visited Monticello and seen the dilapidated condition of the monument, introduced a bill for the preservation of Mr. Jefferson's grave. The bill was passed, with an appropriation of ten thousand dollars for that purpose, provided the family would cede to the government all their right and title to the graveyard. This was refused. In the first sale of Monticello to a Dr. Barkley (who afterwards sold it to Commodore Levy), the graveyard was specially retained by the family. The Legislature of Virginia soon afterwards enacted a law " that no family graveyard should be included in the sale of a place unless by special contract." Thus the government not forcing a quit-claim from the family, it compromised by allowing only its immediate members to be interred there, though retaining control as government property.

The design and construction of the new monument, and its placing in position and enclosure, were intrusted to the Secretary of War, who turned it over to Colonel Thomas L. Casey, Chief of Engineers of the United States Army, who was also assisted by Major Green Peyton Proctor, of the University of Virginia. The new monument is of Virginia granite, quarried near Richmond, Virginia. It is in exact *double* proportions of the original one, having a total height of eighteen feet, including base, plinth, and shaft. The same inscription is cut in sunken letters in the granite, and stands in the same position as the old one, facing the entrance gate. This new monument was begun in 1882, and completed and placed in position in 1883, with appropriate ceremonies. The graveyard is also enclosed by an iron railing seven and a half feet high, with a heavy double iron gate, which is permanently locked.

After the erection of the new monument the old one was placed for a time *outside* the enclosure by the family, that all who desired might obtain a piece, they retaining only the tablet. It was, however, soon after presented to Columbia College, of Missouri, upon the earnest appeal of its board of curators through their president, S. S. Laws, and was removed and placed on the college campus, July 4, 1883, by Professor A. F. Fleet, where it can now be seen, with the original tablet and inscription. We have thus endeavored to give a brief sketch of this handsome tribute by the government to the memory of one to whom this great country is so much indebted, and, being now under the guardian care of a grateful people, it is hoped will never be again desecrated.

A few hundred yards from the cemetery the entrance to the lawn is reached, and a glimpse of the grand scenery spread below is seen. Keeping to the right, we pass the ruins of the celebrated "nail-factory," with its solitary chimney festooned with ivy. Farther on, a solitary grave, surrounded by a stone wall, marks the resting-place of the mother of Commodore Levy, who died here. Next we come to the "weaving-room," which is now the manager's house. Here we are met by a colored porter, who, though looking quite venerable, does not lay claim to being Mr. Jefferson's body-servant, though for a few pennies he will tell you some wonderful stories of him, and point out with pride the many objects of interest. Approaching the mansion up the east lawn, the visitor will stand for a moment and glance at the clock over the door and the weather-vane overhead, which had so often been scanned by the great philosopher. Then reverently entering the double glass doors, he will find himself in the famous hall where Jefferson was wont to meet and greet his visitors.

On the right hangs a full-length portrait of Commodore Levy in full naval uniform; it is a majestic and striking picture of this noted officer; while opposite is a model of the "Vandalia," the flag-ship in which he sailed around the world.

SOUTH-WEST MOUNTAINS

Many other paintings adorn the room which will claim a close and special notice. In the large parlor or *salon* hangs a full-size portrait of Madam Rachel Levy, the mother of Commodore Levy, who was styled the " American beauty" while in Europe, a term not inappropriately given if we may judge by the beautiful features before us. The furniture in this room is of the rich antique pattern, to represent the period of Mr. Jefferson's term as ambassador, while from the ceiling hangs a magnificent chandelier of an old English style for candles. A similar one hangs in the dining-room, both having been imported direct from Europe by Mr. Levy, and are said to have once graced the palace of the Empress Josephine at Malmaison.

The glass doors, the polished floors of parquetry, the antique furniture, and ancient portraits all lend a baronial aspect of the past century in close keeping with its appearance during Mr. Jefferson's time.

The grounds and exterior appointments are well preserved. Scattered over the rich green lawn are rustic benches, statuary, vases, and urns of fragrant plants. Here, beneath stately elms, locust, and chestnut-trees, the visitor can sit and feast the eye upon the vast landscape on every side.

Half a dozen English spaniels sport on the green lawn, while upon the steep, craggy side of the mountain eight or ten deer can occasionally be seen, which are parked by a high picket-fence. The rear, or south-west, lawn is equally as beautiful: from this point is to be seen the mystical looming of Willis's Mountain in Buckingham County,

HISTORIC HOMES

forty miles away, which would be usually pointed out by Mr. Jefferson to his visitors; then to stand on the north-west side of the pavilion and view the university, with the city of Charlottesville spread in the valley below in all its peaceful repose and beauty, while far beyond stretches the vast range of the Blue Ridge, embracing an extent of vision nearly fifty miles in length, which forms a picture such as will repay a journey of several thousand miles to behold.

It is to be doubted whether the government of the United States or the State of Virginia could have done more for the preservation of Monticello than Mr. Levy; being a man of wealth, with an inherited love and admiration for the memory of Mr. Jefferson, he has spared no expense in preserving it in all its pristine beauty, and has expressed his intention of making it one of the great attractive spots in America and worthy the memory of the great apostle of freedom.

Thus it will ever be the delight of thousands from foreign lands, as well as our own sons and daughters, who will visit this historic spot which will remain forever sacred in the hearts of all true Americans.

In conclusion, we can state that Mr. Levy is in no way connected with the Jefferson family; he was named Jefferson Monroe Levy in honor of Virginia's two most noble Presidents, and Virginians will always honor his name in gratitude for his love and patriotism shown in the beautiful care bestowed upon Monticello.

PANTOPS
One of Jefferson's Farms. Now owned by Professor John R. Sampson

PANTOPS

ONE OF JEFFERSON'S FARMS

THE first record we have of the settlement of this noted spot, which stands under the shadow of Monticello, immediately opposite on the north side of the river, we find mentioned in the year 1734, when Jonathan Clarke (father of General George Rogers Clarke), Edmund Hickman, Joseph Smith, and Thomas Graves obtained a grant of three thousand two hundred and seventy-seven acres of land along the Rivanna from "Shadwell branch to Key West." The tract upon which Pantops stands fell mainly to Smith's share and partly to Hickman's. Twelve years afterwards Colonel Peter Jefferson bought a part of this tract, and in 1777, Thomas, his son, purchased the remainder, which had been formerly sold to Charles Lynch.

Pantops was considered one of Mr. Jefferson's "pet farms," and it is said that he hesitated for a time whether his new home should be here or at Monticello, the grand view from this point being hardly less enchanting than its more lofty neighbor.

Pantops—formerly written "Pant-Ops"—was, therefore, so named by Mr. Jefferson from two Greek words, "Πᾶν-'Οράω," meaning "all-seeing," significant of the extended view from its summit.

In 1797, Mr. Jefferson speaks of "opening and resettling the plantation of Pantops," with a view of making it a home for his younger daughter "Polly" (Maria), who had just married Mr. Eppes. But this design was frustrated by the early death of this dear daughter, which event, in connection with impending debts, caused him soon afterwards to part with Pantops, as expressed by a talented writer, "literally for the bread he gave and the wine he poured out for his guests," it passing in settlement of a store account to a merchant in Richmond, Virginia.

This merchant was James Leitch, who married Mary Walker Lewis, the granddaughter of Nicholas Lewis of colonial fame.

In 1803, Mr. Jefferson again speaks of having "levelled" Pantops preparatory to building, and in 1804 writes to his daughter Maria of "levelling and establishing your hen-house at Pantops."

But this hen-house was all that Mr. Jefferson accomplished towards building before parting with the place, and it is said to have been still standing about the year 1877.

The first dwelling-house erected at Pantops was by this James Leitch, about the year 1815. It was a small frame building of two rooms, with a narrow hall through the centre and a long portico in front. After the death of Mr. Leitch, his widow married her cousin, Captain David Anderson, who then added another room at the rear; yet its narrow dimensions could not be styled very commodious, though its proportions were considered quite ample at that time. After the death of Colonel Anderson, his son, Meriwether Anderson, who had married Eliza Meriwether Lewis Leitch, the third daughter of James Leitch, came to Pantops in 1831, where he resided until his death in 1866.

This genial old Virginia gentleman is still well remembered. He was a skilful farmer, a lover of sport and good living, fond of entertaining a host of friends, among whom were Colonel Jeff Randolph, William C. Rives, Franklin Minor, Governor Gilmer, and many others of the *bonhomie* Virginians around him. Under his management Pantops became most productive, and noted for its fine crops, fat mutton, and luscious fruits.

Mrs. Anderson was a lady of great taste and refinement. Her vegetable and flower garden was the envy of her neighbors, and her house always open to the happy gatherings of young people, whom she delighted to entertain. Indeed, Pantops then stood at the apex in the great fame of this region for its hospitality.

In the year 1877, soon after the death of Captain Anderson, Pantops passed into the hands of the Rev. Edgar Woods, who had been pastor of the Presbyterian church in Charlottesville for eleven years. Compelled by failing health to relinquish his charge, he removed to Pantops, and there opened a small school for boys, chiefly to educate his own sons. Such was the success of this small beginning that, upon urgent entreaties of his friends and neighbors for its continuance, he was compelled to greatly enlarge and improve the old mansion of forty years previous, which was even then in sound preservation, though unsuited to modern requirements. For seven years the school continued to flourish under the benignant and wise teachings of Dr. Woods, who, like the great Dr. Arnold, of Rugby, drew young hearts to love him by firm discipline, and gave to youths an impress of character which is still felt by those who were fortunate to fall under his instructions.

Failing health, however, again compelled him to give up his increased labors, and in 1884 Pantops was again sold, with three hundred and seventy-three acres of the original tract, to his son-in-law, Professor John R. Sampson, who had for eight years filled with distinction the chair of ancient languages at Davidson College, North Carolina. Upon taking possession of the school, Professor Sampson found it necessary to again greatly enlarge its facilities to meet the rapidly increased patronage, and at once erected a large three-story building, with all modern improvements for lecture-rooms, study-hall, library, etc., as well as other outside buildings, as dormitories, gymnasium, bathing-rooms, etc., until now the classic summit of Pantops is crowned with many stately and imposing buildings, which, like a "city set on a hill," sends forth its light to all parts of the world, many of its graduates being in foreign lands, while others are filling high and honored positions in our own.

Thus from the small beginning of six pupils by Dr. Woods, in 1877, was founded the present Pantops Academy, an institution which has grown

SOUTH-WEST MOUNTAINS

to national popularity, and such an one as filled the vision of Jefferson when he planned his Central College at Charlottesville, and which would have gladdened the heart of the great advocate for the higher education of youth.

Let us turn genealogically to these two noted families of Woods and Sampson, who have planted such a noble beacon-light of learning on this famous hill. We find the family of *Woods* to be one of the oldest in Virginia, as well as one of the first to settle in Albemarle. They emigrated at an early period from Scotland, settling first at Ulster, in Pennsylvania, and from thence to Virginia. As early as 1734 we find that Michael Woods held large landed possessions near what was long known as Woods's Gap, he being the first to cross the Blue Ridge at that point. He and his sons and sons-in-law were also the first to establish a Presbyterian church in Albemarle, which was then called the "Mountain Plain" Church. His son Andrew was one of the first "Gentlemen Justices" for Botetourt County, appointed under George III. His son Archibald was in the Revolutionary army when not quite sixteen, and was the youngest member of the Constitutional Convention of Virginia, held in 1788. This Archibald Woods afterwards owned sixty thousand acres of land in West Virginia, and founded the first bank at Wheeling, being its president until his death in 1849. His son Thomas was cashier of the same bank, but died while quite young. This Archibald was the father of the Rev. Dr. Woods, the founder of Pantops Academy. It is also an interesting fact that Dr. Woods returned to Albemarle County in 1866, just one hundred years after his ancestor, Andrew Woods, left the county for Botetourt.

The Sampson family is of no less celebrity. We find some of the name as landholders in Goochland County as early as 1725, when Francis Sampson, who is supposed to have been a French Huguenot, took a "patent" which descended from father to son for five generations, or nearly a century, and which was at last sold in 1813 by Richard Sampson and his brothers and sisters.

This Richard lived some time in Albemarle, owning the estates known as Franklin Place, Wilton, and River Bend. He married a sister of the Rev. Thornton Rogers, of Albemarle, a lineal descendant of Giles Rogers, who emigrated from Worcestershire, England, to King and Queen County, Virginia, late in the seventeenth century. His son John married Mary Byrd, the sister of Colonel William Byrd, who obtained a grant of seven thousand three hundred and fifty-one acres of land from Sir William Berkley, governor of the colony, on March 15, 1675, "beginning at the mouth of Shoccoe's Creek," as the deed specifies, and running several miles up the James River, being the present site of Richmond, Virginia. This John and Mary Rogers came to Albemarle, and were the grandparents of General George Rogers Clarke, the famous hero of the Revolutionary war. From his son Byrd Rogers have descended quite a number of preachers: Rev. Thornton Rogers, Rev. Francis S. Sampson, D.D., Rev. Thornton S. Wilson, Rev. Thornton R. Sampson, Rev. Oscar B. Wilson, Rev. William T. Walker, Rev. W. M. Nelson, and Right Rev. Kinloch Nelson, Bishop of Georgia.

Richard Sampson after his marriage with Mary Rogers returned to Goochland and purchased the estate called Dover, which became under his splendid management the most famous plantation in Virginia. The Hon. James A. Seddon, Secretary of War under the Confederate States, who was a near neighbor, writing of him after his death, says in an article to the Richmond *Farmer*, " His transformation of Dover, which was badly impoverished, from a waste to a garden was like a new creation. His plantation was yearly subjected to the inspection of thousands of observers, who were themselves for the most part cultivators of the soil, as the gentry of lower Virginia passed his place on their way to the Springs. It was thus that Mr. Sampson's name soon became a familiar word throughout the length and breadth of the land."

The Rev. Francis Sampson, the son of this Richard, was a brilliant student at the University of Virginia, taking the A.M. He and his roommate, Dennison Dudley, began the first prayer-meeting ever held in the college, the nucleus of what is now the Young Men's Christian Association. They both went from the University to study for the ministry at Hampden-Sidney College, and at the conclusion of his course Dr. Sampson was made there Professor of Oriental Literature. He married Caroline Dudley, a noted beauty, and daughter of Russell Dudley, of Richmond, Virginia. This latter gentleman, with his wife, Mary Baldwin, came early in the century from New England, where both belonged to families distinguished since 1639. The Virginia Baldwins of Winchester and Staunton are from the same ancestors as Mrs. Dudley.

This Dr. Francis Sampson and Caroline Dudley are the parents of Professor John R. Sampson, of Pantops, who married Anne E., the daughter of Dr. Edgar Woods. To this talented and gifted lady is due much of the success of Pantops Academy. Her gentle and loving influence over its more than five hundred pupils who have entered its halls since the year 1884 has left its impress for much good, as evidenced by the numbers of prominent and useful men who have left its walls to battle for the "MASTER" in foreign lands.

During the year 1894 its pupils were drawn from twenty-four States, and Pantopian students were found in thirty-two institutions, from the University of Edinburgh, Scotland, to that of California, nearly all of whom have graduated with high honors.

Thus we see Pantops not only historic in its associations with Jefferson, but eminent as one of the grand institutions of learning in the South, whose well-merited success will ever be the pride and joy of Virginians.

LEGO

LEGO

THE HOME OF THE TAYLORS

ADJOINING Pantops on the east is Lego, another of Mr. Jefferson's famous farms. This was a portion of the nine hundred and eighty-eight acres purchased of Smith and Mosely in 1794. The original farm of Lego contained some five hundred acres, extending chiefly along the steep mountain-sides which stretch even to the river's bank at this point, but, like its neighbor, Pantops, it has long since been shorn of much of its area.

Why Mr. Jefferson gave it the name Lego (I read) is still a debatable question; one story is that he made a colored urchin hold up a book at this spot, while he sat on his lofty Monticello portico, a mile distant, and read from it with his spy-glass; but the most plausible one is that it was in this shady vale, beneath its lofty oaks and beside a cool spring, that he often resorted, and here reclining, with book in hand, would study and dream of the great future for his country. Mr. Jefferson had already erected several log cabins, tobacco-barns, and other buildings upon each of his four farms for the use of his overseers and laborers, hence there was at an early date a small, rude building at the foot of the mountain beside a bold stream which meandered among the hills. About the year 1800, Mr. Jefferson sold Lego to Thomas Walker Lewis, son of Nicholas Lewis and Mary Walker, daughter of Dr. Thomas Walker, of Castle Hill; he built the first framed dwelling at Lego. After several years it again passed to the late Luther George, of Albemarle, who erected the brick portion of the house and lived there until it was again sold to Jefferson C. Randolph Taylor, of Jefferson County, Virginia. Mr. Taylor was the son of Bennett Taylor, a prominent lawyer of Richmond, Virginia, who in middle life moved to Jefferson County and there died. His grandfather was Captain John Taylor, of Southampton County, who was in active service during the Revolutionary war, having equipped and maintained a company of his own. The grandfather of this Captain Taylor was William Taylor, a Scotchman, who is believed to have been the first of the name in Virginia.

Mr. Jefferson Randolph Taylor, of Lego, was a graduate in law at the University of Virginia, and held the position of presiding justice in Jefferson County for many years until his removal to Albemarle. Such was his great integrity of character and sense of justice while holding that position that it brought forth most eulogistic testimony from Bishop Wilmer, of Alabama, and Bishop Whittle, of Virginia, both of whom had been his rector.

Upon taking possession of Lego in 1858, Mr. Taylor added to the original mansion, making it quite large and commodious. He was quite a

SOUTH-WEST MOUNTAINS

successful farmer, this portion of the Jefferson tract having been very fertile, and under his skill and keen judgment it became most flourishing. Mr. Taylor was prominently connected with many important events in the county, and though of a retired nature, yet his opinions were always sought and valued in every movement for the welfare of the people.

In 1838 he married Patsey Jefferson Randolph, second daughter of Colonel Thomas Jefferson Randolph, of Edgehill, grandson of Thomas Jefferson. He died at Lego, January 6, 1878, honored and esteemed by a host of friends for his high standing in all relations of life.

Their children were :

1. Bennett Taylor, who married, in 1865, Lucy Colston; they have six children. He was colonel in the Confederate army, and won distinction as being one of the few to reach the enemy's works during the fearful charge at Gettysburg; he was there taken prisoner and held at Johnson's Island for twenty months. He is now a prominent lawyer of Redford, West Virginia.
2. Jane Randolph Taylor.
3. Susan Beverly Taylor; married John Blackburn.
4. Jefferson Randolph Taylor; graduated at the University of Virginia in the law; is now a minister of the Episcopal Church at Bryan, Texas.
5. Margaret Randolph Taylor; married William Randolph, son of William Lewis Randolph; he died in 1894; she died in 1897.
6. Charlotte Taylor; died an infant.
7. Cornelia Jefferson Taylor; lives at Lego; she is quite talented, and many literary productions have emanated from her gifted pen.

HISTORIC HOMES OF THE

8. Stevens Mason Taylor.
9. Edmund Randolph Taylor.
10. Sydney W. Taylor; died in infancy.
11. J. C. R. Taylor; died an infant.
12. Moncure Robinson Taylor; lives and farms at Lego.

In the year 1894 the old brick building at the foot of the hill, which had sheltered the family so many years, was consumed by fire, but in six months afterwards there arose a large and imposing structure, in the Queen Anne style, upon the crest of the hill (an illustration of which is given). This now forms a fashionable and attractive resort for summer boarders who wish to visit this famous locality.

Lego has always possessed a halo of romance,—its near proximity to Monticello, its lofty hills and shady dells,—it being one of the special resorts of Jefferson in fleeing from the public view,—all of which add to it a peculiar charm. Still more does the grand view expanding from every point of the compass present to the gaze a panoramic picture, embracing the four farms of Jefferson, the South-West Mountain range, the river at its foot, the city of Charlottesville and university beyond, with the Blue Ridge as a background, while on the west rises beautiful Mont-Alto ("high mount") of the South-West range, so named by Mr. Jefferson for its rough, steep sides. This was also one of his farms, containing five hundred and seventy-seven acres, extending even to the celebrated Pen Park farm on the west side of the mountain, where Benjamin Franklin is said to have

SOUTH-WEST MOUNTAINS

visited and made several of his electrical experiments. Mont-Alto was rarely cultivated by Mr. Jefferson himself, being usually rented out, and was eventually sold to his last tenant, Mr. T. H. Craven.

The new building of Lego is capacious, having twenty rooms, with open corridors on every side, where the mountain breezes are continually felt. Its halls are filled with many choice portraits and works of art which have descended as heirlooms in the Jefferson and Randolph families; of these is to be particularly noticed a portrait of Colonel Jefferson Randolph when at the age of sixteen, while studying medicine in Philadelphia. This was painted by the great patriot artist Charles Willson Peale in 1776, who in his admiration for Jefferson presented him with this picture of his grandson, which for many years graced the halls of Monticello. A fine portrait of Sir John Randolph, from a miniature by Bruce, is also here to be seen. It represents Sir John at the time of his visit to England in the interest of William and Mary College, when he was knighted by George II. for his eminent services in the colony. And one of Edmund Randolph, the first Attorney-General of the United States and also governor of Virginia, 1786–88, must not be overlooked. He was the grandson of Sir John Randolph, and his portrait is among the first of Virginia's governors which hang in the State Library at Richmond. The family retain also many relics and documents of Jefferson which are well worthy of notice.

HISTORIC HOMES

In gazing over the vast domain as viewed from its portals, which once belonged to Mr. Jefferson, it is sad to contemplate that Lego is the only spot now owned by any of his descendants which was a part of the original Monticello tract, and even this was only gained by purchase; yet it is linked with the two great names of Jefferson and Randolph, and must ever continue to be of interest to every true patriot of our land.

SHADWELL
The site of the Birthplace of Thomas Jefferson

SHADWELL

THE BIRTHPLACE OF THOMAS JEFFERSON

TWO tall, scraggy sycamore-trees and a few aged locusts are all that now mark the site of the once famous Shadwell mansion, where Thomas Jefferson was born in 1743, O. S.

These are said to be the remains of an avenue of trees which were planted by Jefferson himself on his twenty-first birthday, and are the only silent witnesses of his youthful pranks around the old homestead.

Colonel Peter Jefferson is recorded as having been the third or fourth settler in the neighborhood, and when he began to clear the woods to erect his dwelling he found the trails of the Monacan Indians stretching over the hills.

The story is told that two or three days before Colonel Peter Jefferson took out his "patent" for one thousand acres of land on the Rivanna River William Randolph, his friend and neighbor, had already taken out one for two thousand four hundred acres adjoining; Jefferson, not finding a suitable location for a house on his own land, proposed to his neighbor to sell him four hundred acres; this was agreed to; but such was the friendship between them, and such the abundance of land, that the price paid was to be, as the deed still in the family testifies, " Henry Weatherbourn's biggest bowl of Arrack punch."

In 1737, upon these four hundred acres, situated about three hundred yards from the river, on the northern slope of the hill was built the first Shadwell house, so named after the parish in England where his wife, Jane Rogers (or Rodgers) was born, though others state that it was for *Shadwell Street* in London, where his wife's mother, Jane Rogers Randolph, lived. This celebrated old building is described as having been a plain, weather-boarded house one and a half stories high, having four spacious rooms and hall on the ground-floor, with garret, chambers, and dormer-windows above. At each gable end were huge outside chimneys, which loomed up like gothic buttresses, and massive enough to support the walls of a cathedral, instead of a low wooden cottage. The house sat very near the highway, which then ran along the north bank of the river, and in those days of general hospitality it was the stopping-place of nearly every traveller, who would always be heartily welcomed. Here the great Indian chiefs, who were very fond of Peter Jefferson, would tarry on their journey to Williamsburg, and it was thus that young Jefferson became acquainted with Ontassité, the great Cherokee warrior and orator, and was present in his camp when he made his farewell address to his people before leaving for England. Here Colonel Peter Jefferson lived with his family a happy rural life, gathering in the abundant crops from the rich virgin soil of the surrounding hills, grinding his own corn and wheat, and sawing his own lumber and that of his neighbors at his mill on the river, having little or no expense or care, and little thinking of the great part his young boy Thomas would one day take in the affairs of the nation.

In 1756, Colonel Peter Jefferson died, leaving his estate in charge of his friend and neighbor John Harvie, of Belmont, for the benefit of his only son Thomas, then a youth going to school to " Parson" Douglas, in Louisa County, at sixteen pounds per year, who taught him the rudiments of Latin and Greek, and also the French. He afterwards went to " Parson" Maury, near where Lindsey's old store stood, to whom he paid twenty pounds per session, and of whom he speaks as being "a classical scholar." After graduating in the law, young Jefferson, then having attained his majority, assumed control of the estate, and carried on the farm as in his father's time, at the same time he entered upon the practice of his profession in the courts of Albemarle and surrounding counties. It was while absent attending some distant court that the old homestead was destroyed by fire in 1770, after which it was never rebuilt. The loss to young Jefferson by this occurrence was very great, consuming a valuable library and many papers and records of his father's long and active life in the county, which would have thrown much light upon its early settlement and history. The story is told that when a servant was sent to tell him of his loss, he asked at once if any of his books and papers had been saved. The old darky replied, with some satisfaction, " No, massa ; nothing but de *fiddle!*" Mr. Jefferson was devoted to music, and the old negro thought that the violin was esteemed the most valuable article of all.

Mr. Jefferson now turned to the little mountain, in full view on the other side of the river, though distant four miles off, as a site for his new home. The spot is still shown on the river bank where he kept his canoe, and would daily paddle himself across, clambering up the steep hill-sides to where he was levelling the apex of the mountain preparatory for building. But there was much yet at Shadwell to claim his attention, and had he been content to rebuild upon the old site, it would have resulted better for his fortunes. Here at the foot of the hill stood his grist- and flour-mill, the stone walls of which are still to be seen, while its site forms a rich garden spot which can be viewed daily by passengers on the Chesapeake and Ohio Railway. Here, too, were situated many of his tobacco-barns, stables, and out-buildings for his numerous slaves, forming quite a settlement of themselves. And here, too, were timber and material in abundance for building at comparatively little expense ; but the far-off grand eminence of the little mountain had a peculiarly attractive influence upon his ambitious spirit, which seemed prophetic of that great eminence he would attain in the hearts of his countrymen.

It was in after-years that, notwithstanding Mr.

SOUTH-WEST MOUNTAINS

Jefferson's removal to his new home, Shadwell rose to importance as a manufacturing town, rivalling even its neighbor Milton on the south side. In 1835 it contained a large carding-factory employing nearly a hundred operatives, a large merchant mill under the management of Messrs. John Timberlake & Son, a saw-mill, and several stores, shops, and dwellings, all stretched along the north bank of the river. The river was then navigable to this point, and here were shipped the grain, tobacco, and products of the surrounding country, as well as large quantities of flour and cotton-yarns, which would be floated down the river in long bateaux. These were busy, halcyon days for Shadwell. The musical toot of the boatman's horn or his merry song of

> "Inspiring bold John Barleycorn,
> What dangers thou canst make me scorn!
> Wi' tippenny we fear no evil,
> Wi' esquibac we face the devil!"

would often resound along the steep Rivanna cliffs. Even so late as 1850 it continued to be quite a commercial place; but in that year the carding-factory was destroyed by fire, and though frequent efforts were made for its rebuilding, this was never done, its ruined walls standing for many years as a monument of its departed glory, and after the advent of the railroad Shadwell rapidly declined. Here, along the banks of the river, was the great highway for stage travel in those days, which crossed the river at Secretary's Ford, near the present railroad iron bridge, or farther up at Pirea, upon the bridge there built by "Billy" Meriwether at a cost of four thousand dollars, which always bore his name. At times "Billy" would get into contention with the stage lines as to toll-rates, whereupon he would rip up the planks of his bridge until the stages would come to terms or risk the fording at high water.

The river at Shadwell would often get on a rampage, flooding the mills, stopping travel, and doing much damage. Mr. Jefferson always recorded these events, which to him meant a serious loss; still, he always averred that the water-power at Shadwell was the best, and his design was to extensively utilize it, making here a great manufacturing town.

In 1879 the site of the old Shadwell mansion with two hundred and thirty acres of land, being a portion of what was called the "Punch-Bowl tract," was sold to Mr. Downing Smith, of Greene County. In 1880, Mr. Smith erected a small two-story frame dwelling not far from the site where the old Jefferson house stood, the two old sycamore-trees being immediately in front of it, one on each side of the road leading to the house.

Mr. Smith married Willianna Minor Marshall, the daughter of that sterling old Virginia farmer, Captain James T. Marshall, of Oakland, near Milton. Mr. Smith's grandfather was Downing Smith, of Madison County, and his father, also named Downing, of Greene County, both of whom were prominent and successful farmers. Mr. Smith has inherited much of their talent and energy, as is evidenced by the fine crops annually produced on the old Shadwell place. This farm was considered by Mr. Jefferson the best of the four which he owned and cultivated on both sides of the river, and Mr. Smith has proved the fact that the rich fields immediately surrounding the old mansion were those from which Mr. Jefferson made most of his wheat and tobacco.

Mr. Smith now owns ten hundred and thirty-five acres of the original Shadwell and Edgehill tracts; of the latter he has five hundred acres called Underhill, which lies between two spurs of the mountain, not far from the Edgehill mansion. The house is almost hid by its dense foliage and secluded position, having an extensive lawn which forms quite a sylvan retreat. This place was once called Slab City by Colonel Jeff Randolph, doubtless from the fact that here were made most of the pine slabs used for building purposes in old times, which were manufactured from the heavy mountain timber.

At what period the house was built or by whom is not known. This tract has been cultivated by many of the Randolph family, the last of whom to own it was Miss Sarah N. Randolph, the talented authoress.

Mr. Smith has since been offered a handsome sum for Shadwell, but which has been declined, he wishing to erect a handsome building in the near future, beautifying and adorning the old site, and preserve carefully the venerable trees, which

HISTORIC HOMES

are now objects of great interest. It is to be hoped, however, that a suitable monument will be erected here by the State, marking the birthplace of her great son, that in connection with his home at Monticello it may be preserved imperishably as one of the historic spots within her borders dedicated to his memory.

SHADWELL THE SECOND

SITUATED on an elevated hill near the base of the South-West Mountains and nearly opposite the old Shadwell site, which is two miles distant, stands a commodious brick building, much in style of the Edgehill mansion. This was erected nearly fifty years ago by Colonel 'Frank G. Ruffin, who married, in 1840, Cary Anne Nicholas Randolph, third daughter of Colonel Thomas Jefferson Randolph, of Edgehill. This he named Shadwell, after the old Jefferson birthplace, though the station and post-office on the river still retained the name, which has since been removed to the Edgehill Station.

Here Colonel Ruffin lived and raised a large family. He proved himself to be one of the most astute farmers and able writers upon agricultural matters of the day, following closely in the footsteps of his illustrious father, Edmund Ruffin, who so long and ably edited the *Farmers' Register*, which gave to agriculture in Virginia an impulse which it has never ceased to feel. After the death of Colonel Ruffin this part of the Shadwell tract, which originally contained nine hundred acres, was sold to Major Thomas J. Randolph, Jr., the eldest son of Colonel Jefferson Randolph, of Edgehill, who took possession in 1830, and lived here till his death in 1870, which was caused by an accidental premature blast on the Chesapeake and Ohio Railway in West Virginia, where he had a contract. Major Randolph married twice: first, Mary Walker Meriwether, the daughter of Dr. Frank T. Meriwether; and second, Charlotte N. Meriwether, daughter of Dr. Thomas Meriwether, of Kinloch, by both of whom he had several children, some of whom are still living on the old Meriwether estate.

After the death of Major Randolph this part of the Shadwell tract passed into several hands, until eventually sold to Mr. V. A. Bunch, of Huntington, West Virginia, who is its present owner.

There are now but one hundred and twelve acres attached to the house, the remainder of this once large tract having been cut up into small farms and sold to strangers, who have erected buildings upon many of its prominent points.

This second Shadwell building is not so ancient in appearance, nor possessed with mysterious legends of old; yet the fact of its being the last part of the Jefferson tract to be sold, and with it the passing from the family all of the once famous " Punch-Bowl tract," will ever render it of peculiar interest.

EDGEHILL

THE HOME OF THE RANDOLPHS

EDGEHILL stands next to Monticello in historic celebrity, and its early history and settlement are coexistent with that of its neighbor Shadwell. It is one of the few places that was first settled when the county of Albemarle formed a part of Goochland, and the South-West Mountains marked almost the extreme western limit of habitation.

As has already been mentioned, William Randolph, of Tuckahoe, Goochland County, in 1735 patented from the crown of England two thousand four hundred acres along the South-West Mountains, adjoining the lands of Peter Jefferson on one side and John Harvie on the other.

But William Randolph, of Tuckahoe, never built nor settled upon this large estate himself; it was his son, Colonel Thomas Mann Randolph, who was the first of the family to settle there in 1767. At this time the Randolphs were very large land-owners, their estates extending from tidewater to the mountains, and their name was recorded in the earliest annals of the colony. We read first of this Colonel Thomas Mann Randolph as a very prominent supporter of the church, it being recorded that in 1720 he erected an entire church building, fifty by twenty feet in size, at his own expense, costing fifty-four thousand nine hundred and ninety pounds of tobacco; and again it states that a tax of three pounds ten shillings was levied on the parish to defray the expenses of consecration of the Rev. Mr. Griffith as bishop, of which sum Mr. Randolph paid three pounds. This Colonel Randolph also had a large estate at Varina, on James River, which he left to his son, Colonel Thomas Mann Randolph, Jr., who was Mr. Jefferson's son-in-law, but, as we shall presently see, he spent very little of his time at Varina, being compelled to remain at Edgehill.

Edgehill (always spelled by Mr. Jefferson with a small h) was so named by Colonel Randolph for the field near the village of Edgehill, in Warwickshire, England, where the Cavaliers under Charles I. first crossed swords with the Roundheads in 1642. As Colonel William Randolph, of Turkey Island, James River (the first of the family in Virginia), emigrated from Warwickshire, England, in 1651, soon after that exciting event, we may presume that Colonel Randolph, of Tuckahoe, thus named his new home in honor of his grandfather, who had doubtless lived near the great battle site. It is said that the view from our present Edgehill much resembles that of its English namesake, which gently slopes to the south, the battle having been fought on the declivity of the hill.

In 1790, Thomas Mann Randolph, Jr., afterwards governor of Virginia, built a large frame dwelling near the site of the present Edgehill mansion, and after his marriage with Martha Jefferson resided here most of his time. The house was then quite commodious and far better than those generally built at that day.

Mr. Jefferson had always been anxious to have his son-in-law settle near Monticello. In 1791 he writes, " I hope Mr. Randolph's idea of settling near Monticello will gain strength, and no other settlement in the mean time be fixed upon. I wish some expedient may be devised for settling him at Edgehill." Thus Mr. Jefferson exerted his efforts to have this building erected so that his daughter might be near him.

When Colonel Thomas Mann Randolph, of Tuckahoe, came to Edgehill he was a widower, having lost his first wife, the daughter of Colonel Archibald Cary, of Ampthill, Chesterfield County, Virginia, who was the mother of his eldest son, Colonel Thomas Mann Randolph, Jr. When this son won and married the beautiful and gentle daughter of his neighbor on the right (Mr. Jefferson) the father turned to his neighbor on the left, and sought the hand of the fair and fascinating Gabriella Harvie, the daughter of Colonel Harvie, of Belmont, who, by pressure of her parents, gave her hand to Mr. Randolph, though her heart is said to have been with poor Marshall, her father's clerk. So it was that the father and son lived at Edgehill with their young wives peacefully and happily. Mrs. Gabriella Randolph is described as being a woman of great beauty and fashion, who made the Edgehill mansion a continual scene of festivity and lavish entertainments; but this did not last many years, as the father soon afterwards died, leaving Edgehill to his son, Thomas Mann Randolph, Jr., who, in 1819, became governor of Virginia, and in 1825 a Presidential elector. It is reported that as soon as young Marshall heard that Mrs. Gabriella Randolph was a widow he again sought her hand, but this time, upon receiving a very cold reception, he disappeared, and was never heard of again. Mrs. Randolph afterwards married Judge Brokenborough, of the Warm Springs, Bath County, Virginia.

Governor Randolph is described as being "tall and graceful in person, renowned in his day as an athlete and for his splendid horsemanship; having a head and face of unusual intellectual beauty, bearing a distinguished name, and having an ample fortune, any woman might have been deemed happy who was led by him to the hymeneal altar." Mr. Jefferson also speaks of him as "a man of science, sense, virtue, and competence, in whom, indeed, I have nothing more to wish."

Edgehill now became almost equal to Monticello as a resort for the many distinguished visitors who came in the neighborhood. There the governor entertained the celebrated Portuguese botanist Correa, roaming with him over the South-West Mountains in search of American specimens; also Leslie, the naturalist, and many others from Europe, who would come first to see Mr. Jefferson, and then be taken to Edgehill and the surrounding plantations.

SOUTH-WEST MOUNTAINS

Mr. Jefferson was so very tenacious in having his children and grandchildren around him that they spent most of their time at Monticello, and it was not until after his death, in 1826, that Governor Randolph and his family made Edgehill their permanent home. Previous to this Mr. Jefferson had placed most of his business and farming affairs in the hands of his young grandson, Thomas Jefferson Randolph, for whom he had formed a special attachment, and who spent most of his time at Monticello. In a letter written about the year 1815 he says, "I am, indeed, an unskilled manager of my farms, and, sensible of this from its effects, I have now committed them to better hands, of whose care and skill I have satisfactory knowledge, and to whom I have ceded their entire direction."

Soon after this Governor Randolph died, leaving to his eldest son, Thomas Jefferson Randolph, the management of the Edgehill estate, upon whom had already devolved that of Monticello and the other farms of Mr. Jefferson, which for a young farmer of twenty-three was somewhat of an undertaking, but which was accomplished with a skill and judgment such as would have befitted one of many years his senior. In 1828, Colonel Thomas J. Randolph, finding the old family dwelling at Edgehill far too small for his growing family and the modern requirements of the day, removed the old building a short distance to the rear, and erected upon its site the front part of the present brick mansion.

As an incident in connection with this removal, it is stated that there stood three or four young poplar-trees immediately in its rear, around which it was impossible to move the building, and not wishing to cut them down, they were bent down, and the house was made to go over them, and to-day these trees are still standing in all their gigantic strength and magnitude.

In 1836, Mrs. Jane Nicholas Randolph, the wife of Colonel T. J. Randolph and daughter of Governor W. C. Nicholas, opened a small private school for the education of her own daughters and those of her relatives and friends, there being few desirable female schools at that time. She was gifted in an eminent degree for this undertaking, and such was its success that it was continued. This was the beginning of the Edgehill School, an institution which has since gained so justly almost a national reputation.

At the death of Mrs. Randolph the school was continued by her eldest daughters, Misses Mary B. and Sarah N. Randolph. The war then coming on, it was discontinued until the year 1869, when it was again resumed and kept up without interruption until the year 1896, when it was finally closed.

In the early seventies the school increased so in numbers that it was again found necessary to enlarge its capacities, especially in its art and musical departments, and this was done by utilizing the original frame building, which still stands in all its quaint appearance and undiminished strength of nearly one hundred years ago.

SOUTH-WEST MOUNTAINS

After Miss Sarah N. Randolph established her famous school at Patapsco, Maryland, and later in Baltimore, the Edgehill Seminary was conducted by Miss Caroline R. Randolph, assisted by her nieces, Misses Mary W. Randolph, Eliza Ruffin, and Jane R. Harrison. The latter, as Mrs. Randall, is now the principal of a flourishing school in Baltimore.

The happy influences exerted by the daughters of Colonel Randolph, who inherited in a marked degree the fine intellectual qualities of their grandmother, Martha Jefferson, who had been so carefully educated by her father in Paris, have left their impress upon and formed some of the most lovely female characters of our land. Aside from its high literary standard, the Edgehill School always exerted a fine salutary, *home* influence upon its various pupils. They were taught the great value of possessing true womanly traits of character, and in this and other directions the example of their preceptors was of incomparable value.

In fact, too high tribute cannot be paid to the intellectual attainments, high character, and great industry of these Randolph ladies. Within the precincts of their beloved home they have fought the hard battle of life quietly but heroically, and have given the world a royal example of what toil and perseverance can accomplish under circumstances the most adverse and trying. When Colonel Randolph nobly assumed the debts of his grandfather, Mr. Jefferson, it practically ruined him financially, and when later on he sustained still further losses by the civil war, his financial condition became most desperate. It was in this dark hour that his heroic daughters came to the rescue, and by lives of sacred devotion to duty succeeded in lifting the heavy responsibility from their father's shoulders and saving the devoted homestead from passing into the hands of strangers. The world pays but scant tribute to these long, fierce, silent battles, and in so doing slights the noblest portion of its heroes and loses the far better part of its heroism.

Besides the duties so faithfully performed in school and home, Miss Sarah N. Randolph found time to write her most excellent " Domestic Life of Thomas Jefferson," and also a " Life of Stonewall Jackson." The former work portrays with loving touch the exquisite inner life of our great statesman, and in consequence must ever stand as one of the noblest monuments to his memory.

Beautiful Edgehill will always be a noted spot, not only for its grand scenery, its extensive lawn, and park of majestic forest-trees; its productive fields, which in 1856 produced six thousand bushels of wheat, at two dollars and twelve cents per bushel, and fourteen hundred barrels of corn; its large gardens, which have become famous for their productions; its grand mansion filled with relics of Jefferson; its walls adorned with fine paintings, many of which are from the hand of a talented granddaughter, but more than all for being the home of one of Virginia's ablest governors, and more recently that of his son, Colonel Thomas

Jefferson Randolph, than whom there was no man more devoted to the interests of his county and State, and whose services, we fear, have not been duly appreciated by the present generation. As a single incident in his busy life, and one well worthy of note in view of after-events, he introduced a bill in the Virginia Legislature, while a representative from Albemarle County, prior to the civil war, *looking to the gradual emancipation of the slaves of the South.* The times were not ripe for such a move, however, and the bill, with its enormous possibilities for good, failed of passage.

In 1876, Colonel Randolph, as the representative descendant of Mr. Jefferson, was chosen to open the Philadelphia Centennial, but died just a few weeks before the inauguration of that famous event.

There are many who remember him as a most notable man, tall in stature, with a commanding and dignified presence, with a countenance and traits of character very characteristic of Jefferson, with a fund of humor and anecdote most captivating in conversation, and a store of information which he was always ready to impart. His opinions were always given clearly and forcibly, and were received with satisfaction and delight by his many friends ; his keen sense of justice and right combined with the beautiful character of a most humane and gentle master, around whom his old slaves were wont to cluster and remain even after their freedom,—such was the recent master of Edgehill, of whom much more could be said, but must be reserved for a more able pen.

HISTORIC HOMES

Nor must the visitor, as he glances over the beautiful landscape which stretches forth on the southern horizon like a vast sea, while stately Monticello and Carter's Mountain loom up to the west, with the Rivanna winding among the hills at its feet, lose sight of the "Edgehill Memorial Chapel," which sits on the gentle slope of an adjacent hill. This tasty little Gothic structure, with its stained windows and modest belfry, will ever be associated with Edgehill as a monument to the pious work of the various teachers and pupils of its famous school. To one of the beloved inmates of Edgehill in particular, however, is due much of the success of this sacred undertaking, and already the beneficent effects of her gracious labors are felt far and wide throughout the surrounding countryside.

Much of this once large estate has been sold and is now occupied by strangers, but the mansion, with several hundred acres, is still retained by the family, and must ever remain one of the noted historic homes of Albemarle, and be classed with those of Montpelier, Pen Park, Castle Hill, and others, which, it is hoped, will always be preserved to perpetuate the simple domestic lives of their great men.

Edgehill will not only be dear to the hearts of Virginians, but also to the very many in the far South who have spent there so many happy days amid all that is pure, refined, and elevating.

BELMONT

THE HOME OF THE EVERETTS

CONTIGUOUS to Edgehill, on the summit of a gentle hill crowned with lofty cedars and oaks, once stood the Belmont mansion, which for its stately proportions, unique architecture, and beautiful symmetry had no counterpart; but let us turn a leaf backward before attempting to describe it.

In our notice of Edgehill we have already mentioned Colonel John Harvie, who was the friend of Colonel Peter Jefferson. We find that this Colonel John Harvie (or Harvey, as sometimes given) was of Welsh stock. He came to the county about 1730, and bought about the same time as his neighbor, Colonel William Randolph, of Tuckahoe, two thousand five hundred acres of land from a certain Joshua Graves, lying east of the Edgehill estate, and embracing the present farms of East Belmont, Springdale, Keswick Station, Broad Oak, and Everettsville.

At the death of Colonel Peter Jefferson we find him the guardian of young Thomas, who, in a letter about the year 1760, consults him as to his education; again, in 1790, Mr. Jefferson mentions Mr. Harvie as possessing a good tract of land on the east side of Edgehill, which he was exceedingly anxious for his son-in-law to buy, but for some unaccountable reason old Harvie refused to make him a deed, though having at first consented. This disappointed and irritated Mr. Jefferson very much, who had, while governor of Virginia, appointed Colonel Harvie register of the land office. It was while holding this position that his young clerk, Marshall, fell in love with his daughter Gabriella, but who was compelled to marry Colonel Thomas Mann Randolph.

Dr. Brokenborough, of the Warm Springs, who was at one time president of the Bank of Virginia, and who afterwards married the gay widow Randolph, thus speaks of Colonel Harvie: "Colonel Harvie in early life was a lawyer in Albemarle, a delegate to the Virginia House of Burgesses, and was appointed jointly with John Walker a commissioner to treat with the Indians at Fort Pitt. He was then chosen a member of the old Congress, and afterwards elected register of the land office of Virginia, which was a wealthy position. He resigned this, and was elected a member of the House of Delegates from the city of Richmond, serving two years. He died in 1807 at his seat Belvidere, near Richmond, leaving seven children, none of whom were living in 1845 but General Jaqueline Harvie and Mrs. Brokenborough, then in her seventy-eighth year. Colonel Harvie's son died young; his son, John, married Miss Hawkins; his son, General J. Harvie, married the only daughter of Chief-Justice Marshall; his son, Edwin, married Miss Hardway, and died in the burning of the Richmond Theatre. Mrs. John Harvie lived many years after her husband's death, most of her family having perished in the burning of the theatre in 1811.

"It is said that Mrs. Gabriella Brokenborough, when her husband failed in business while in Richmond, sacrificed her home, furniture, plate, jewels, and all in her efforts to save him."

Previous to his removal to Richmond, Colonel Harvie had placed his property in the hands of his friend John Rogers to be sold, and in 1811, Dr. Charles Everett, of Albemarle, purchased twelve hundred acres of the Belmont tract, while John Rogers retained and lived upon the portion of the estate known as East Belmont.

The original house, thought to have been first built and occupied by Colonel John Harvie, was then standing in good condition, though considered a very old building. It had nine small rooms, was one-and-a-half stories high, with wings at each end, and high dormer-windows, giving it a very antique appearance.

Here Dr. Everett lived and entertained his intimate friends and neighbors with cordial hospitality. He was a man of great talent in his profession, reserved in disposition, and possessed of an indomitable will. Rather suspicious of men in general, he was yet warm-hearted and liberal when their sincerity was proved, and consequently was slow in making friends, but very tenacious in holding them. He was a keen observer of human nature and its various workings, and often used the knowledge thus gained to the surprise and benefit of his many patients. Save in a few instances he was a disbeliever in medicines, and held that the physician's highest aim should be to assist Nature rather than coerce her.

He graduated in medicine at the University of Pennsylvania in 1796, and, with a short interruption, continued the practice of his profession until his death.

The break in his medical career mentioned occurred in 1817, when he became the private secretary of President Monroe, and afterwards a representative in the State Legislature from the county of Albemarle. Soon quitting politics, he returned to his profession, and in a short time became one of the most famous physicians in the State. Besides Albemarle, his practice extended over seven adjoining counties, and at one time he was called to attend Bishop Madison in Richmond. He was also one of the consulting physicians in the last illness of President Jefferson. Though they were such close neighbors they were far from being very close political friends,—Whig *vs.* Democrat,—and even the little friendship they had nearly vanished when Jefferson looked up, and, seeing Dr. Everett one of the three, said, with a touch of grim humor, " Whenever I see three doctors I generally look out for a turkey-buzzard !" and, though Jefferson meant it as one of his jokes, the sensitive doctor took it seriously and hastily withdrew.

He had a horror of pretence and quackery in all forms, and never failed to deal either a blow when occasion called for it. Being besieged once by a long-winded plough agent and having endured the fellow's persistency until patience ceased to be a virtue, he said, "No, sir, I do not care for your plough; I am well supplied at present." "But, doctor," continued the plough vender, "if you don't need it now, you will need it some day." "Yes, you —— rascal; and I will need a coffin some day, too, but I don't propose to buy one now."

Upon one occasion he was called in to see a notorious old miser who had fallen into a profound stupor from which nothing could arouse him. After several unsuccessful efforts, Dr. Everett noticed the county sheriff passing by, and, remembering his patient's ruling passion, went out and, hastily summoning the official, told him to come into the sick man's chamber and drop his saddle-bags upon the floor with a loud rattle, as though they contained a goodly quantity of specie. This the officer did, and as soon as the jingle subsided, Dr. Everett said, "Mr. Sheriff, how much money did you say you had collected for Mr. Jones here?" Before the sheriff could reply, the old miser stirred on his couch, his keen eyes opened slowly, and in a voice made husky with eagerness he cried, "*How much did he say?*"

Dr. Everett numbered among his personal friends some of the most prominent men of the day,— Madison, Monroe, Hugh Nelson, Bishop Madison, Benjamin Rush, Francis Walker, Alexander Stevenson, James Barbour, Francis W. Gilmer (one of his wards), John C. Calhoun, and Governor Nicholas.

The Hon. Francis Walker, of Castle Hill, appointed him as guardian of his daughters, one of whom, Judith Page Walker, afterwards married the Hon. W. C. Rives, and was the grandmother of Amélie Rives (now Princess Troubetzkoy), the authoress.

Dr. Everett died in 1848 at the age of eighty-one. His portrait by Naegle, a pupil and son-in-law of Sully, hangs on the walls at Belmont, and is highly prized for its artistic execution and life-like resemblance.

As an evidence of its excellence in this latter respect, it is said that when the portrait was first brought from Philadelphia after the death of Dr. Everett it was immediately recognized by his faithful house-dog, the fond creature even going so far as to rear against the wall beneath it and bark loudly, as though in joyous welcome at the return of its long lost master.

A fine crayon portrait of Dr. Everett in early manhood, by Saint-Memin, is also preserved and highly prized at Belmont.

Dr. Everett left the vast bulk of his large estate, amounting to about two hundred and fifty thousand dollars, to his nephew, Dr. Charles D. Everett, of Philadelphia. His will directed that his many slaves should be freed, and that they should be transported to Liberia and there settled in furnished homes. Besides this provision for their shelter, one thousand dollars were given to each family as a start in the new life.

Dr. Everett, Jr., becoming convinced that the

wilds of Africa were unsuited as a home for these helpless, ignorant people, took advantage of a codicil to the will giving him discretionary power upon this point, and carried them to Mercer County, Pennsylvania, for settlement.

Dr. Charles D. Everett, who succeeded to the Belmont estate, was a Kentuckian by birth, though a Virginian by descent, his ancestors having settled in Williamsburg in 1650. His father, expecting to become an Episcopal minister, had received an excellent education, but, early giving up the sacred calling, had joined the then free and popular ranks of the "old Virginia planter." At the time of his marriage he was a wealthy resident of Rappahannock County, Virginia, but, alas! following the custom of the times, he went security for a number of friends, lost nearly everything he had, and finally decided to move to the "wilds" of Kentucky, in the faint hope of recouping his fallen fortunes.

He found the country utterly uncleared, but thinly populated, and almost entirely without the conveniences of civilized life. His nearest neighbors were five or ten miles distant, his mill and post-office even farther removed, schools were practically unknown, and before a single crop could be planted the virgin forests had to be cut down and the land cleared up. Wild animals roamed the woods freely, and it was not an uncommon occurrence for the settlers to be chased by large packs of wolves.

For pecuniary reasons, a return to Virginia was

impossible, so the new settlers determined to make the best of the situation, and accept with equanimity the many attendant hardships.

It was amid such scenes as these that Dr. Charles Everett first saw the light. He was born in 1806, and his life from his earliest youth was an extremely busy one. His father, accustomed to the ease and luxury of a Virginia planter's life, found it, not unnaturally, almost impossible to accept the new order of things, and consequently, as the years went by, the support of his large family fell almost entirely upon the shoulders of his eldest son. And nobly did the son perform the onerous and sacred duties.

At length, his younger brothers growing up, he was enabled to leave home and begin the great battle of life for himself. Owing to the circumstances and surroundings of his birth and early youth, his acquired advantages for the contest were naturally few; but he possessed those innate qualities of heart and brain which always win success, no matter how long and bitter the conflict may be.

Early deciding to be a physician, he at once bent every energy to the acquisition of means for that end. Refusing the proffered aid of his wealthy Virginia uncle, he entered the strife single-handed. Of course the battle was the usual fierce one, wherein privations, hardships, and uncongenial employments played their usual prominent parts, but the great goal was constantly kept in view, and the end was happy, for in 1836 he graduated in medicine from the University of Pennsylvania, and soon thereafter began to practise his profession in the city of Philadelphia.

At the time of his uncle's death in 1848 he had secured an excellent practice, but his health being very poor in the city, and the large interests of the vast estate left him demanding his immediate presence in Virginia, he determined to move thither at once and settle permanently on the fine old estate of Belmont. This he did in the early part of 1849, taking up his abode in the old Harvie house, which was still standing in excellent repair.

The writer can well remember the building when upon one occasion the gay and handsome doctor gave a party to which the entire neighborhood was invited, having the famous Scotts (old Jesse and his two sons Bob and Jim) as musicians, and such music they made as the gods of Terpsichore will never hear again in this generation,— such music as caused the old chateau to rock and reel to the cadence of the tripping feet and made old hearts young again!

After the marriage of Dr. Everett, in 1852, to Miss Mary Coleman, of Nelson County, Virginia, he determined to erect a new building more in accord with the progress of the times and in consonance with his refined taste for modern architecture, therefore, in 1858, the old house was moved to the rear, dividing it into two out-buildings, and upon its site the new mansion was built.

This was of brick, stuccoed in imitation of stone. It was about sixty feet in length by forty-five in width, and rose to the grand height of fifty feet from the ground. It was crowned by a lofty roof, the summit of which was enclosed with handsome iron railings and used as an observation tower.

The building was three stories in height, its rooms being of magnificent size and pitch. The entrance to the front hall was gained by a lofty flight of granite steps, flanked on each side by massive abutments, on the top of which were parterres of blooming flowers and stately plants.

The wide porticos were supported by majestic pillars, having cast-iron capitals of Corinthian design. The double front doors opened into a grand hall twenty feet wide, forty-six feet long, and twenty-five feet in height. In the southern end of this apartment a handsome gallery was constructed, and in the northern end an immense window reached from the floor to the ceiling. Just in front of this window a pretty fountain played, its jet falling into a marble receptacle for goldfish. This hall was designed by Dr. Everett for dancing, with the gallery for musicians; but it was seldom used for that purpose during his lifetime, though it was often the scene of other gay and festive occasions. Running at right angles to this hall were side corridors on each floor, built especially for the staircases and as connecting passage-ways between the front and rear apartments. Besides these corridors and the superb hall the house contained thirteen large rooms, and the usual number of store-rooms, closets, etc. On the first floor were the dining- and dessert-rooms, the bath-room, library, and kitchen. On the second, the parlor, the reception-hall, and three bedchambers. On the third, four bedchambers and the gallery before mentioned.

The immense windows on each side reached from the second floor to the eaves of the building, their lofty columns being surmounted by arched iron frames, giving a pleasing and most graceful effect.

A large tank in the roof of the building, holding fifteen hundred gallons, and filled by a ram nearly a mile distant, supplied the house with hot and cold water. The building was heated by a furnace in the basement and fireplaces in each room, and thus its appointments were most complete in every respect. This handsome structure cost seventeen thousand five hundred dollars, and was three years in building. Certainly no country house equalled it at that day, as it then stood the pride and ornament of the neighborhood.

Here Dr. Everett lived a happy, useful, noble life, entertaining liberally his hosts of friends, helping the poor and needy at every turn, dispensing gifts of charity with unstinting hand, encouraging the progress of the arts and sciences, especially as applied to agriculture, horticulture, and the mechanical arts. He was a man of great scientific research, and would put many theories into practical shape to the great benefit of his neighbors.

When the civil war came on it found Dr. Everett of an age which exempted him from actual service, yet he put in a substitute, and also took his place in the ranks of the little "Home Guard" beside his more humble neighbors. Such was his intense devotion to the Southern cause that he fitted out an entire company with arms and uniforms at his own expense. His house was always besieged by passing soldiers, none of whom ever left his door during those dark days without being most liberally fed and entertained. It was here that General Jubal Early made his head-quarters at one time during the war; and when the appeal rang forth for money and help during the last sad struggle of the expiring Confederacy, he cheerfully lent the government one hundred and ten thousand dollars, none of which, it is needless to say, was ever returned. Such peerless deeds as these should be recorded as in marked contrast to the sordid, money-grabbing spirit of the present day, and with the hope that our youth may be stimulated to perpetuate such true patriotism.

After the war Dr. Everett continued to exert himself in "doing good" and in building up the shattered fortunes of his State. We find him frequently teaching the ignorant blacks, or as a faithful superintendent of a Sunday-school, or the president of an agricultural society, or in whatever position placed he exemplified a noble, true Christian character.

Dr. Everett died in 1877, gently passing away in the noble mansion which he had reared and adorned with his own hands, and it was not many years after when it, too, passed away.

SOUTH-WEST MOUNTAINS

It was Sunday, the 11th of March, 1883, while the family were at the little "South Plains" church, two miles distant, that the top of the building was seen to be on fire. It had caught from sparks on the roof during a high wind. The building being very prominent the fire was quickly seen, and neighbors from a distance rushed to the rescue, hoping to save the house, but this was impossible, as the entire top was quickly a mass of flames.

As soon as Mrs. Everett reached the house she calmly walked into the burning building, and with a presence of mind such as few would possess under such circumstances she secured most of her valuable papers and jewelry.

Again the old chateau, now fully two hundred years old, remodelled and moved back upon its ancient site, is doing good service by sheltering the family, its timbers as sound as ever, surrounded by stately elms and Kentucky coffee-nuts, lofty poplars, and the graceful Green Mountain ash, which was brought from Vermont as a small switch in his trunk by the elder Dr. Everett and planted by him where it now stands a giant tree.

From the summit of Belmont the visitor can enjoy a view of magnificent and surpassing beauty and such as the hills along the South-West Mountains alone can afford; but a sigh of deep regret will ever escape from the many who can remember the once stately Belmont mansion, which formed one of the happiest as well as the most picturesque homes along this famous region.

HISTORIC HOMES

The ten children of Dr. and Mrs. Everett are:

1. Alice Kate, born December 16, 1852; died August 2, 1871.
2. Mary Coleman, born December 13, 1854.
3. Clara, born October, 1856; died April 6, 1859.
4. Louise Montague; married Charles Landon Scott, a prominent lawyer of Amherst County, Virginia, August 26, 1885. They have eight children.
5. Charles Edward, died October 1, 1887.
6. John Coleman, physician in Nelson County; married Nellie Martin, of same county, August 26, 1885. They have four children.
7. Aylette Lee; married Miss Sadie G. Fry, of Albemarle, January 24, 1888. Have three children living.
8. Hettie Hawes.
9. Joseph William; manages the Belmont Farm.
10. Alice Harrison.

EAST BELMONT

THE HOME OF ISAAC LONG, ESQ.

THREE families of prominence have resided at East Belmont,—Rogers, Thurman, and Long,—each of which claim our attention as being among the first to locate in Virginia.

Mention has already been made of John Rogers, the friend of Colonel John Harvie, of Belmont, who, in 1811, sold to the elder Dr. Everett the greater portion of that tract. The remainder of this extensive plantation, which contained more than two thousand acres, Mr. Rogers bought himself, and built there the frame part of the present mansion, now owned and occupied by Mr. Isaac Long. His great friendship for old Dr. Everett, and the constant and close intimacy between them, led "Farmer" John (as he was universally called) to retain the name of Belmont ("beautiful mountain") by simply adding the word East, to show its position. It is said that previous to settling here he made a trip out West with a view of locating there, but after wandering over many States he concluded that there was no fairer section in the country than Albemarle, so, returning, he selected the beautiful stretch of table-land at the foot of Hammock's Gap. We have already given a sketch of the Rogers family in the notice of

Pantops, from whom this "Farmer" John is a direct descendant, and like his contemporary Richard Sampson, of Goochland, won much celebrity as a farmer, and was known throughout the State for his skill and success in agriculture. After his death the estate fell to his son John, who married a Miss Sampson, also a direct descendant of Richard Sampson, of Goochland, and sister of the late Stephen F. Sampson. This John Rogers, Jr., built the brick addition, or front part of the house, as it now stands, and greatly improved the place. It is also remarkable to state that all the brick of the house were burnt and laid by a colored workman named Lewis Level, he doing nearly the entire work himself, the substantial quality of which still shows a skill not usually found among negroes.

This was one of the very few brick buildings then erected along the mountains, and was quite conspicuous. John Rogers, Jr., lived here for many years, a most prosperous farmer and most influential citizen. At his death his widow and her two sons, Thornton and William, retained the place, it being worked for several years by her brother, Stephen F. Sampson, who, with his sisters, also lived there. About the year 1840 Mrs. Rogers married Edward Thurman, of Tennessee, after which Mr. Sampson moved to Springdale, an offshoot of Belmont, which was located at the foot of the gap.

"Farmer" John had also another son, named Thornton, who was a Presbyterian clergyman, and

SOUTH-WEST MOUNTAINS

who married Miss Margaret Hart, the sister of the late James Hart, of Fruitland, the adjoining farm. The lower part of the East Belmont farm was then cut off and given to this Rev. Thornton Rogers, who built there his home called Keswick, located near the county road. He also built the "South Plains" church upon a part of the land below the road, and was its pastor until his death, thus establishing one of the first churches of that denomination in Albemarle.

Edward Thurman, who married the Widow Rogers, was descended from the prominent Thurman family who have figured so largely in the political history of our country, some of whom were among the first settlers of Albemarle, and fill an interesting page in its history. The first of the name in America was Benjamin Thurman, who, with his brother, settled on the north side of the South-West Mountains about the year 1732. His brother afterwards moved to Campbell County. The house which Benjamin Thurman first built stood not far from where the road passes over the mountain at Hammock's Gap. From Benjamin Thurman descended the Rev. Pleasant Thurman, and through him Allen G. Thurman, who was chief justice of the Supreme Court of Ohio, Senator from Ohio, and was the Vice-Presidential candidate in 1888 with Mr. Cleveland. He also received the nomination for governor of Ohio three times, but which was declined each time.

Benjamin Thurman had built his house and was living at Hammock's Gap as early as 1734, and was said to be living there as late as 1825. He married Miss Carr, a lady of rare intelligence and education. She is said to have written some very fine verses, specimens of which are preserved in the family to this day; they were chiefly hymns, all of her poems being of a religious character, many of which were adopted by order of the " church" and sung regularly in " meeting."

Hammock's Gap derives its name from a hunter whose cabin stood just in the gap. Some of the property which Benjamin Thurman obtained came through this William Hammock as assignee, His Excellency Governor Henry Lee, of Virginia, having signed the documents in the year 1792, and another patent from George II. was signed in 1734 by William Gooch, then governor of the colony.

Tradition says such was the religious fervor of Mrs. Benjamin Thurman that when she visited her distant neighbors in the valley below before leaving them she would gather the household—whites, slaves, and all—for singing and prayers, in imitation of the disciples.

From Benjamin Thurman descended Elisha Thurman and Dr. Fendall Thurman. Elisha remained here, and lived on the top of Wolf Pit Mountain, now known as Edgehill Mountain. He owned the entire mountain, with adjoining lands on the north side. The old house in which he lived has long since been removed, and no vestige of it remains except the stone fence which surrounded the garden and the walls of the cellar. The name of the mountain (Wolf Pit) was given from a large pit made by this Elisha Thurman in rear of his corn-house to catch the wolves and other wild animals which frequently depredated upon his sheep. The spot is still pointed out by knowing ones, and is also referred to by Dr. G. B. Goode in his excellent address made before the United States Geographic Society in 1896 at Monticello. He says,—

"I have myself seen in this locality pits partially filled up which were used as wolf-traps not half a century ago, and have talked with a man whose father had seen a herd of buffalo crossing Roanoke River, less than two hundred miles south-west of Charlottesville, called Buffalo Ford."

In 1743 wolves and buffalo were still abundant along the mountains, and the inhabitants were accustomed to collect bounties in tobacco for their capture. The stream called Wolf Trap Branch, near Charlottesville, also preserves the memory of those times.

On the highest point of Wolf Pit Mountain is a spot called View Rock, from which is obtained one of the most extensive prospects in Albemarle, embracing in panoramic scope nearly the entire county, extending from Liberty Mills in Madison County, with the entire interlying valley reaching far beyond Charlottesville, to Gordonsville in Orange County, and on the south as far as the eye can reach into Nelson County, all of which can be seen without moving one's position on the rock, embracing also a view of more than fifteen miles of the Rivanna River as it winds among the foot-hills.

It was from these steep mountain sides that the entire supply of firewood for the University of Virginia was once obtained before the advent of coal. The marks of the graded road from Pantops to its summit are still to be seen which was used by Colonel " Jeff" Randolph and Elisha Thurman in drawing the wood to the college, they having obtained the contract for its supply.

Dr. Fendall Thurman, the younger son of Benjamin Thurman, emigrated early to Memphis, Tennessee, and there amassed a fortune by trading with the Indians and practising his profession. Before leaving Virginia he married Miss Ann Royster, daughter of David Royster, of Goochland County, whose wife was Elizabeth Sampson, sister of the famous Richard Sampson who lived at the elegant old Virginia homestead Dover, of which we have already written.

From this union descended Edward Thurman, of East Belmont. The wife of Elisha Thurman is said to have been also very religious, and frequently opened her house on top of the mountain for preaching, there being no church building nearer than the court-house at Charlottesville, which was then used by all denominations. She also organized the first Sunday-school in the county at her house.

In 1817, it is stated that John Thurman, George Walker, and James McGee formed the first Sabbath-school in the State in the Methodist Episcopal church at Lynchburg.

SOUTH-WEST MOUNTAINS

Mr. Edward Thurman lived at East Belmont for many years, becoming a most successful farmer and prominent citizen. The famous old farm under his management maintained its former reputation for large crops, yielding frequently five thousand bushels of wheat in one season, which would be sold at two dollars per bushel, and other crops were in like proportion, gaining for East Belmont the celebrity for being the most productive farm along the South-West Mountains.

In 1879, Mr. Thurman sold eight hundred and eighty-eight acres of this fine tract to Mr. Isaac Long, of Page County, Virginia, leaving still about four hundred and fifty acres of the original farm, which had previously passed to the Springdale and Keswick farms on each side of it. East Belmont fell into hands no less distinguished than its owners of the past. Mr. Isaac Long is the son of the late Isaac Long, Sr., who was born at and lived on the Old Fort Long homestead, the large estate of which was originally acquired under the English crown in 1720 by his paternal ancestor, Philip Long, who was one of the first to settle in the Shenandoah Valley of Virginia. Here he died at the age of sixty-two, being one of the most prominent and influential men of the county of Page, and was celebrated as a most successful farmer.

His son, Isaac Long, the present owner of East Belmont, married, in 1856, Elizabeth H. Mohler, eldest daughter of Colonel Jacob Mohler, who came into possession of the noted Weyer's Cave of

HISTORIC HOMES OF THE

Augusta County in 1834, it having been held by the Mohler family for many years. Colonel Mohler was a direct descendant of Ludwig Mohler, of Switzerland, who came to America in the good ship "Thistle" in 1730. The Mohlers first settled in Pennsylvania, the house which John Mohler built in 1764 is still standing near Ephrata, Pennsylvania.

Colonel Mohler lived at Weyer's Cave for many years, and was widely known as the proprietor of this wonderful freak of nature, which he was the first to open to the public.

Colonel Mohler was also distinguished for being an officer in the Mexican war, a man of great integrity of character and learning, and a stanch Methodist and temperance advocate. In 1846 he moved to Page County, where he lived until his death, which occurred in Baltimore, Maryland, at the advanced age of seventy-six.

Mrs. Elizabeth Mohler Long, of East Belmont, is also closely related to many of the most eminent families of Virginia, the Mohlers having intermarried with the Grigsbys, Andersons, McCormicks, McNutts, Hamiltons, and Hickmans, each of which have given the State many illustrious characters, among whom we may mention Hugh Blair Grigsby the historian; General John Warren Grigsby, of the Confederate army under General Joe Wheeler; Captain Reuben Grigsby, of the United States army in the war of 1812, and also a member of the Virginia House of Delegates; General Joseph R. Anderson, of Richmond, who graduated at West Point, was in the Florida

SOUTH-WEST MOUNTAINS

war, and afterwards established the Tredegar Iron-Works, of Richmond, Virginia; Governor William McCorkle, of West Virginia; Dr. James Gardener Hickman, of Missouri, who gave to Henrietta Hamilton McCormick the celebrated powder-horn carried by Alexander McNutt at the battle of the Cowpens, in the Revolutionary war; Leander James McCormick of "Reaper" fame, whose father, Robert McCormick, began the manufacture of his great invention on a small scale in Virginia, but which after his death was improved upon by his son Leander, who moved to Chicago in 1846, where, with his brother Cyrus, he built up one of the greatest establishments in the country. It is this Leander McCormick who gave the large telescope and observatory to the University of Virginia.

Though proud of such distinguished kinship, which richly entitles her as a "Daughter of the Revolution," yet Mrs. Long is of a most retiring disposition and reluctant to boast of her noble ancestry. Some of these celebrated men have honored East Belmont with their presence, thus adding to its historic fame of the past.

Mr. Isaac Long for a number of years was magistrate for the county of Page, and also served the county for two terms in the Virginia House of Delegates.

Since coming to Albemarle he has devoted himself entirely to agriculture, making many improvements to the East Belmont farm and reaping from its rich fields most bountiful crops.

HISTORIC HOMES

The children of Mr. and Mrs. Isaac Long are:

1. J. Ernest Long, of Orange Court-House, Virginia; married, November 26, 1890, Nannie Watson, of Green Springs, Louisa County, Virginia.
2. Laviece Long; married, June 28, 1892, Harvie Sibert, of Sedalia, Missouri.
3. Linda F. Long; died young.
4. Lula Latrobe Long.
5. Isaac Trimble Long; married, December 19, 1891, Ada White, of Leesburg, Virginia, now of Fairfax County.
6. Bessie Mohler Long.
7. Frances Blair Long.
8. D. Grigsby Long.
9. Margaret Long; married, January 2, 1897, Robert Adelbert Dewees, of Del Rio, Texas, now of Chicago, Illinois.
10. James Carroll Long.
11. Thomas G. Long; died young.

It is needless to say that these bright sons and daughters have served to make East Belmont very charming and attractive, especially as their parents have been wont to keep up the old hospitable style of the valley, in good living, bounteous cheer, and much festivity, which has made their beautiful home the scene of many bright gatherings, which will always linger in the hearts of those who were fortunate to be among the happy participants.

SUNNY SIDE
The Summer Residence of J. B. Pace, Esq., of Richmond, Virginia

SUNNY SIDE

THE SUMMER RESIDENCE OF J. B. PACE, ESQ.

THIS place originally was a portion of what was once known as Clark's tract. Dr. Micajah H. Clark, the eldest son of Major James Clark, here first lived and built quite a good-sized frame building, which was early established as a tavern, being situated immediately upon the stage-road leading from Charlottesville to Gordonsville; here were also located extensive stables for the relay of horses, thus affording quite a market at that time to the surrounding farmers for their abundant crops of hay and grain. With its many out-buildings and daily business enterprise the place assumed quite the appearance of a small village, hence it was called Clarksville, a name which it long retained. The tavern itself was first conducted by Miss Bettie Clark, the sister of " Kid Clark of the Pines," who is said to have been quite a stirring old lady, who ran the business much to her own liking.

Dr. Micajah Clark, who was then quite a prominent physician, evidently married twice, though the " Meriwether Family" book states only one union; but if we visit the old Clark burying-ground in the " Pines," near which the site of Kid Clark's house is still to be seen, we will there find a solitary marble slab bearing the following inscription:

> "CAROLINE VIRGINIA CLARK,
> Infant daughter of
> Dr. Micajah Clark
> and
> Caroline Virginia Clark.
> Born Novr 21st, 1831,
> Died Septr 15, 1832."

This Caroline Virginia must have been the first wife of Dr. Clark, and presumably died soon after their marriage. He married secondly, Margaret Sampson, of the same family as his neighbor Stephen F. Sampson.

After living here a short time he and his family moved to the West, where many of his children settled and married.

Clarksville then reverted to his eldest daughter, Anne M., who married Colonel Richard Watson, of the Green Springs, Louisa County, Virginia. Colonel Watson continued the old tavern during the forties, and did quite a large business with the stage lines; after this he removed to Charlottesville and conducted for a number of years one of the university boarding-houses, after which he retired to his farm, Poplar Forest, near Milton, where he died. This genial and popular gentleman was truly one of those strikingly attractive Virginians of the past of whom we now read much of, but who are rarely to be seen.

After his death Clarksville was inherited by his eldest daughter, Jane M., who married William

SOUTH-WEST MOUNTAINS

H. Fry, of Richmond. Mr. Fry did not reside at Clarksville very long, as the civil war coming on he moved to Richmond, where he engaged largely in business and became one of its prominent citizens.

Just previous to the breaking out of hostilities Clarksville was rented to a Northern gentleman named Furslew, who was quite an eccentric character, being extremely fanciful in his ideas of farming and beautifying the place, which he began by forming a large lake near where the present one is, and filling the lawn with many kinds of shrubs and flowers quite new to this section, and laying out plans for improving the farm upon the Northern system; but the war coming on frustrated his designs, his sympathies being altogether antagonistic to the South, he therefore quickly sold his household possessions at a sacrifice and suddenly left.

Clarksville was then occupied during the war by Mr. Wilson Summerville, a refugee from Culpeper County. This hearty, jovial, old Virginia gentleman made it a very pleasant place during those sad days. Though well in years he was as active as a youth, and during a festive night would dance with all the spirit of a boy. Clarksville, however, had always been a merry place, where dancing was wont to be displayed in the true old Virginia style; the vivid picture of its then owner, William H. Fry, cutting the double and triple pigeon-wing in the Virginia reel is still in the eye of the writer.

HISTORIC HOMES OF THE

After the civil war Clarksville was bought by Mr. Michell, an Englishman, who, under the firm of Vaughan, Michell & Co., had also purchased the large farm of Fruitland, where they attempted English farming on Virginia soil, but which proved ineffective. This gentleman began to make the first real improvements which have so changed its appearance. The old tavern was made to assume a more modern aspect by the addition of a large rear wing, and with other enlargements it formed quite a cosey English chateau, where much hospitality and cultivated refinement were shown.

It became an attractive place for the many English residents who had been drawn to this beautiful part of Virginia. Here they would frequently gather and enjoy with true English spirit the many games and amusements of the old country.

After the signal failure of Messrs. Vaughan, Michell & Co. in their farming enterprise, Clarksville reverted to Mr. Fry, who then sold it to Mr. James B. Pace, of Richmond, Virginia, its present owner.

Upon taking possession of Clarksville, Mr. Pace at once began its real transformation into one of the handsomest places along these beautiful hills. The old Colonial building which had so long been familiar to the public view was now entirely snuffed out by having a stately two-story edifice built completely over it, and when finished the little, low one-story dwelling was pulled to pieces and thrown out of the windows of the new build-

SOUTH-WEST MOUNTAINS

ing, which towered so far above it. The lake which had been begun by Furslew was greatly enlarged, having islands connected by rustic bridges, with arbors amid a wealth of foliage, around which floated miniature gondolas, giving it truly an Oriental aspect. The lawn and adjacent grounds were most artistically laid out with beds of many variegated flowers and shrubs, while a spacious greenhouse on one side afforded a rich variety of tropical plants. Altogether the embellishments of the grounds alone cost seventeen hundred dollars, while the total expense of the place, with its large barns, stables, and extensive gardens, its wide fields, each bordered with rows of trees, and the many outside improvements, has been more than twenty-five thousand dollars. Certainly no country-seat in Virginia is more complete in all its appointments than Sunny Side, which was so renamed for its bright and cheerful aspect and the sunshine of many happy days there spent by joyous youth.

Thus it still stands in all its beauty, which is largely due to the skill and taste of Mr. Henry Brown, an English landscape gardener and florist, who for many years had charge of the place, and has shown what Virginia farms can be made to assume under the art of scientific and skilful management.

In the midst of this immense growth of noble oaks and stately evergreens sits the spacious mansion which is almost hid from view, affording that retired seclusion so delightfully enchanting to rural life, and which gives to Sunny Side a peculiar charm. Here the expenditure of wealth and art has gained not only pleasure and comfort to its inmates, but has instilled a higher sense of beauty and culture to others who are striving with laudable ambition to make their homes more picturesque and beautiful, and to discard the careless and improvident system of a past age.

Mr. J. B. Pace is one of the few self-made men of Virginia who have risen from a plain farmer's boy to great wealth. He was born in 1837, his father being Granville T. Pace, a successful planter of Henry County, Virginia. With few advantages of education he entered quite early into active business, and when but fifteen years of age began to actively engage in the manufacture of tobacco. In 1858 he moved to Danville, Virginia, and married that year Miss Bessie Neal, daughter of Mr. Thomas D. Neal, of Halifax County, Virginia. Mr. Neal had married Miss Carter, daughter of the celebrated Samuel Carter, who, it is said, never bought anything for his family but tea, coffee, and sugar, all else for the table or to wear being made on his large plantation.

Mr. Pace continued in the manufacture of the leaf at Danville for several years in connection with his father-in-law, Mr. Neal, until 1865, when he moved to Richmond, where he greatly enlarged the tobacco business. During the war Mr. Pace could not take an active part owing to ill-health and a delicate constitution; but he became a most liberal contributor in aid of the Confederate cause, and when the end came he found much of his

SOUTH-WEST MOUNTAINS

hard-earned fortune swept away; but with the same energy which has marked his career he began again the tobacco business upon a much larger scale, which soon attained gigantic proportions, causing his success to be most marked and rapid.

Few men have gained so early in life such eminence in business circles, or commanded such confidence among influential men, and though meeting with many reverses, yet his constant energy and continued success seemed unimpeded until it reached into the millions. Much of the beauty and improvement of Richmond is due to Mr. Pace. Besides many private residences he has erected several large public buildings which are an ornament to the city and give it a commercial influence.

Nor must we lose sight of her whose quiet liberality and sympathetic feeling for suffering humanity go hand in hand with her public-spirited husband, dispensing of their wealth most liberally among the various Christian institutions as well as the poor and needy in private walks of life.

The children of Mr. and Mrs. Pace, nine in number, are:

1. Nannie; married Mr. Donnan, of Petersburg, Virginia. Died July 29, 1881.
2. Violet; married the Right Rev. Milville Jackson, Bishop of Alabama. Died in Richmond, 1893.
3. Thomas; died in 1886, aged twenty-one years.
4. Carrie; married Mr. W. W. Hite, of Louisville, Kentucky, January 4, 1888.
5. James.
6. Bessie.

HISTORIC HOMES

7. Edgar.
8. Mary Carter; married Mr. Robert Newell Groner, son of General Groner, of Norfolk, Virginia, February 15, 1897.
9. Ethel Randolph, so named in honor of the Misses Randolph, of Edgehill Seminary, who educated the three eldest daughters, Nannie, Violet, and Carrie.

Mr. Pace has given his children every advantage for the highest education, sending three of them, James, Carrie, and Bessie, to Europe, where they had the opportunity of the foreign schools of art and science.

FRUITLAND

THE RESIDENCE OF A. P. FOX, ESQ.

THE historic interest of this place lies in the fact that here was once the home of the *Clark* family, whose name is interwoven with that of Lewis, in connection of their many brilliant deeds during the early period of our country.

The Fruitland tract lies between East Belmont and Cismont, embracing at one time the present Sunny Side and Cedar Hill farms, and was very early known as Clark's tract, which extended from the summit of Sugar-Loaf Mountain to far below the present county road. This large area was taken from the famous Meriwether tract under the king's patent, as we find Elizabeth Meriwether, the daughter of Colonel Nicholas Meriwether, of Clover Fields, married Thomas Walker Lewis, and their daughter, Margaret Douglas Lewis, married James Clark, an officer in the Revolutionary army, who afterwards settled at Fruitland.

But the first settlement made upon the tract was by Kid Clark, the father of this James Clark, who built a small house near the mountain, at a spot known as the "Pines." The site of his house is still to be seen near the boundary-line between Fruitland and Cismont farms. This first dwelling was standing in 1811, but upon taking possession of Cismont Mr. Peter Meriwether moved a portion of it to his own place, where it now stands as one of the oldest relics of the past. Previous to this Major "Jimmie" Clark, as he was generally called, had built the Fruitland house, the rear part of which shows its great antiquity.

At first this place was called Ben Coolin, a name only found in the island of Sumatra; but as the Clark family were of Scotch origin, "Ben," signifying mountain, and "Colyn" or "Coolin," the Scotch term for "breezy," we can readily see that its early settlers gave its name for some lofty hill in Scotland meaning "Breezy Mountain," being most appropriate to the Fruitland location, which rises from the plain to quite a prominent elevation, which makes captive the mountain breezes from every point.

Major Clark lived for many years at Fruitland, raising a family of two sons and four daughters. About the year 1830 he sold the farm to John Carr, who lived on top of the mountain, and started for Missouri, with his wife and children, on his sixtieth birthday, but did not long survive the tedious journey, as he died in St. Louis in 1838. Major Clark was a near relative of General George Rogers Clarke, the "Hannibal of the West," who died in Kentucky in 1817, also to William Clarke, his brother, both of whom were born in Albemarle, not far from Charlottesville. Their father also moved to Kentucky, and settled, in 1784, upon the present site of Louisville.

SOUTH-WEST MOUNTAINS

All of the Clark (or Clarke) family have been prominent in our country's early history; and whether they are descended through Robert Clark, who is first mentioned in Virginia history in 1728, or from the New England Clarkes, Thomas Clarke being the mate of the " Mayflower," is not clearly shown, but the name, whether spelled with the final " e " or not, is believed to be of the same stock, whose descendants are now to be found in every State of our broad Union.

John Gay Carr lived at Fruitland some years and then sold it to the late James Hart, who married first, a Miss Harris, and second, Mrs. Frances Meriwether *née* Frances E. Thomas, of Kentucky. Mr. Hart became a most successful farmer, realizing large crops from his extended fields, and, like its neighbor East Belmont, the Fruitland farm became noted for its waving fields of hay and droves of fat cattle. Mr. Hart gave its present name of Fruitland for its large orchards of fine fruit, some of the apple-trees of fifty years ago still bearing their luxuriant crops of luscious fruit.

After the death of Mr. Hart Fruitland was sold to a company of Englishmen, who made the first payment with the expectation of completing the full purchase from proceeds of the farm; but English farming was found not quite applicable to Virginia, and after one or two years of failure it was again sold, and purchased by Mr. A. P. Fox, a retired merchant of Richmond, who had married one of Mr. Hart's daughters.

Though coming with little or no experience as

HISTORIC HOMES

a farmer, yet Mr. Fox has greatly improved the mansion, and by his skill and energy made Fruitland to yield its bountiful crops as of old. The cooling summer breezes still waft through its old oaks surrounding the now modernized mansion, alluring to their pleasant shade many visitors from the heated cities. Here one can view from its summit the peaceful valley below, studded with handsome residences, having the village of Keswick and the Chesapeake and Ohio Railroad nestled at its foot, while in the distance sits the village of Cismont on the one hand, and Monticello on the other,—truly a picture most enchanting.

In 1850, Mr. Hart gave his eldest son the northeastern portion of the farm, upon which he built quite a portentous brick building, which sits on the summit of one of the highest detached hills from the mountain. This place he named Cedar Hill, for its many cedars which crowned it. But he lived here only a short time, selling it in 1856 to Mr. H. A. Burgoyne, of New York, and since 1863 it has passed through several hands, its present owner being Mr. J. N. Black. The interest in this spot centres upon a small frame house which once stood at the foot of the hill beside a bold spring, which was surrounded by lofty poplars and many fruit-trees. Here lived an eccentric old man named De Foe, who kept a little grocery, and the legend is told that Mr. Jefferson frequently stopped here on his journeys to Washington to stir up a toddy and talk politics with the old man.

CISMONT
Summer Home of Colonel H. W. Fuller, of Washington, D.C.   Remodelled 1895

CISMONT

THE SUMMER HOME OF COLONEL H. W. FULLER

IF there is any place where joy, happiness, and peace have truly dwelt, where youth and old age have spent happy hours of the past, and where the true Virginia type of hospitality and royal good living were to be seen, that place is Cismont, now the beautiful home of Colonel H. W. Fuller, so widely known as the general ticket agent of the Chesapeake and Ohio Railway system.

The first settlement of Cismont dates back to a period beyond the ken of the present generation.

In 1800 there stood an old frame building, one and a half stories, at the foot of the hill, on the summit of which the present mansion stands. This old building was very ancient in appearance, and even then was considered of centennial date, as its peaked roof and rickety boards fully attested. There it sat nursed and cradled among the surrounding hills for so many years. Near its doorstep flowed a clear, bold spring, which still gives forth its crystal waters, while lofty oaks, pines, and poplars sheltered it from the noonday sun. Long lines of fruit-trees bordered the lane which led to the public road, while luxuriant fields of waving grass, wheat, and corn betokened the virgin richness of its soil. It was a cosey and inviting spot as it then stood, in all its rude surroundings of that real old Virginia period when exteriors were considered of less importance than interior comforts. Such was the first Cismont house, though tradition says that there have been five dwellings erected on different parts of the farm, and one " meetinghouse," which latter stood near the little stream which passes at the foot of the hill. On this stream, near a large rock still to be seen, was a deep pool of water used for baptizing, which was called " Grandma's" from the fact of so many old people being baptized there. At this spot was baptized Miss Betty Clark, the sister of Kid Clark. She was called " Aunt Betsy," and kept the tavern at Clarksville (now Sunny Side) for many years.

Previous to this, however, the old Cismont house is said to have been used also as a tavern, kept by a man named Moore, and, as it stood not far from the county road, the daily stages would sweep up to its door for passengers to partake of the good cheer within while exchanging horses.

About the year 1820, Peter Minor Meriwether came here to live with his young bride, Mary Walker Meriwether, the eldest daughter of Captain William D. Meriwether, of Clover Fields, who, as we shall see, owned all the lands from this point to Belvoir, being a part of the original Meriwether tract, which extended to the Turkey Sag road.

It is said that while courting his pretty " Cousin

SOUTH-WEST MOUNTAINS

Polly" he became so discouraged that he threatened to leave Virginia for the far West; this decided at once the fair lady, who consented on condition that he would live here. Captain Meriwether then gave them four hundred acres of the Clover Fields tract, upon which the old tavern stood. In 1824, Mr. Meriwether added several small tracts, and in 1841 purchased of his father-in-law more than two hundred acres lying on Sugar-loaf Mountain, thus making the total Cismont farm six hundred and forty-one acres. Mr. Meriwether was a direct descendant of David Meriwether, the fourth son of Nicholas Meriwether (2d), and grandson of Nicholas (1st), the first of the name in America.

They are said to have been English Quakers and once spelled the name "Merryweather." They had the personal friendship of George II., who bestowed upon the first Nicholas Meriwether a grant for more than eleven thousand acres of land, most of which embraced the South-West Mountains, and extended into Louisa and Fluvanna Counties. When we come to describe the homesteads of Clover Fields and Kinloch we will enter more fully into their history, which forms one of the most interesting chapters in the early settlement of this historic region.

The new home was saddened by the death of Mrs. Meriwether in 1832. In 1836, Mr. Meriwether married Mrs. Frances W. Tapp, of Oak Hill, near Stony Point. About this time he also began to erect a new dwelling upon the top of the hill, which he named Cismont. The brick for this building was burnt and laid in 1836 by a celebrated mechanic named McMullin, who built about the same time the Edgeworth house and several others in the county. At the completion of this new house in 1837, the fame and glory of Cismont began: its noted fertility, the overflowing hospitality of its owner, the vivacity and charming grace of its mistress, combined to give it a celebrity such as few places possessed.

But before we enter upon the gay scenes of the new mansion, let us glance again at the old chateau under the hill, whose attractive scenes still linger like a bright halo of dreamland, as memory reverts to its old halls, its winding stairs, and intricate chambers.

In 1841, after the removal of Mr. Meriwether and his new bride to the more imposing building on the hill, which was always called the "Big House," the old tavern was occupied by the Rev. E. Boyden, who had just come to the neighborhood as the rector of Walker's Church parish. He gave it the name of "Cottage Rectory," and in 1845 opened there a small school under the tutelage of Mrs. Eleanor Richardson, of Richmond, Virginia, to whose gentle, patient, untiring efforts is due the transformation of the wild, unsophisticated boys and girls of that period into models of gentle men and women. Mr. Boyden also conducted quite a flourishing fruit nursery, introducing many new varieties of the apple, which have since become famous for this region. Thus with the

SOUTH-WEST MOUNTAINS

"Rectory School" and its joyous band of youth, and the many visitors to the beloved pastor, made the "Cottage" home a continual scene of mirth and pleasure, notwithstanding that its walls were said to have been *haunted*, and its many dark nooks and corners the abode of spooks and hobgoblins. This belief was doubtless from the fact of many deaths having occurred there, which superstition served a good purpose in governing wayward boys and girls, who would be threatened with the "dark closet." Among the many visitors to this happy circle was one eccentric genius, who always afforded much merriment; this was George Jeffery, an English teacher, engaged at Dr. Mann Page's school. He had decided merit, having attended Cambridge, in England, but his many antics and peculiarities gave the impression of his having been either a comic actor by profession or a *crank* of the first water. His chief forte was the singing of comic songs, accompanied by many gestures and contortions of countenance, which would keep his young audience in fits of laughter or exert real terror. On one occasion a servant-girl who was serving the table at which he sat laughed so much at his oddities that she went into convulsions and died.

This remarkable character is mentioned in the "Page Genealogy;" he was very irritable, getting into many scrapes, and soon after returned to England, much to the regret of the young people. In 1849 the "Rectory School" was discontinued, and in 1850 Mr. Boyden moved to his new home near the church. After this the old house went to decay, and in 1860 was torn down.

We will now turn again to the new Cismont mansion as it then stood. It was a plain, unpretending two-story house, having six rooms, with a hallway in the centre and a long portico in the rear; around it were scattered the usual farm buildings, while the yard was filled with young elm- and cherry-trees, together with various kinds of shrubbery, many of which were brought from England. It was not its exterior surroundings which then gave such a charm and attraction to Cismont, but the genial, loving hearts of its master and mistress which was the magnet that drew so many to its doors.

Mr. and Mrs. Meriwether were perhaps more widely known, loved, and respected than any two persons in the county. Both were young, with an extensive kindred and large acquaintance; it was come and go at all times, and "Cousin Fanny" and "Cousin Peter" with everybody; or even the more endearing titles of "Aunt" and "Uncle" or "Mother" and "Father" would be used by those who had been recipients of their loving-kindness. They were ever ready to open wide their doors for the young people to have a frolic; he with his violin would add the charm of music, while she would set out the abundant stores of her larder. No wonder the house was always full; no wonder the stranger as well as the kinsman would linger and be loath to step away from that charming spot; and thus it would be for weeks at a time.

SOUTH-WEST MOUNTAINS

But it was Christmas that the real merry-making began. Then the rollicking and frolicking of the young people reached its climax, when young and old, white and black, had a real good time. Preparations would begin weeks beforehand,—the jellies, cakes, puddings, and pies would be piled in heaps in the cellar below; the slaughtered fowls and meats were ready; huge casks of cider and bins of luscious apples were in waiting; and when at midnight of Christmas-eve the darkies would fire off the big log charged with powder, and blow the old ox-horn, and would raise a great shout, then every one knew that Christmas had come, and the fun would begin. The sun would hardly be above the horizon before neighbors would begin to pour in to greet "Cousin Fanny" and "Uncle Pete" with happy Christmas and to partake of eggnog and an early breakfast. The young boys and girls would also soon troop in with merry greetings, and then the old fiddle would be drawn forth and the dancing begin. These were the times when it was "open house, free and easy" to all,—the latch-string was always hanging out, the best of eating and drinking was on the outspread table, and roaring fires made the good cheer within. Around the festive board would frequently be gathered some of the most brilliant and happy spirits of the past,—the courteous William C. Rives, the sententious Franklin Minor, the always smiling F. K. Nelson, the benignant Rev. E. Boyden, the benevolent "Uncle" Jimmy Terrell, the blunt "Uncle Dick" Gambill, the hearty Dr. Tom

Meriwether, and the witty "Billy" Gilmer; and here, too, would frequently be seen "Aunt Betsy" Meriwether and "Aunt Sue" Terrell," or graceful Mrs. J. P. Rives and her gentle sister, Mrs. Jane Page, or "Aunt" Sarah Gilmer and Mrs. A. M. Mead, and thus they would come and go, all welcomed and all made happy. But while the "old folks" are eating and cracking their jokes the young folks are tripping to Mr. Meriwether's violin accompanied by the piano. There they are, a merry crowd,—Stephen Sampson and William H. Fry (then young boys) are cutting the pigeon-wing and swinging around Sarah Campbell and Sally Watson; Tom Randolph and Mary Walker, Bill Lewis and Fanny Campbell, George Geiger and Charlotte Meriwether, Fred Page and Ann Meriwether, and dozens of others,—there they all go in the merry dance, their voices ringing forth shouts of laughter. Nor do they stop until the smiling "Aunt Frances" steps in to announce supper, and then they scamper down the narrow stairway to the cellar below, the boys frequently squeezing the girls or taking a sly kiss on the way. And then the good things quickly disappear, when they again scamper back to have games, candy-pulling, and fortune-telling, and so the fun continues to a late hour of the night. Nor is the festivity and frolic confined to the "big house," for the negroes, little and big, are having a grand time, with plenty of hog meat and fat chittlings, sweet 'taters and 'tater pumpkin, flour cake and apple pies, rousing wood fires and no work, all in sharp contrast to the present daily struggle under freedom. Such is a picture of the good old times at Cismont, a time the remembrance of which causes the heart to sigh as it exclaims,—

> "When I was young? Ah, woful when!
> Ah for the change 'twixt now and then!"

Mr. Meriwether was a most peculiar man. He was a true type of *Meriwether*, being firm of opinion, quick in judgment, bold and fearless in expression. His habits, manners, and general appearance would often mislead the casual observer as to his true nature. Being an intense Jeffersonian Democrat, he would, when twitted by his opponents on his political heterodoxy,—his apostasy from the true *Whig* faith, his ugly locofocoism,— express his opinions most dogmatically, without regard to the niceties of diction and in language more forcible than elegant, and, like the great John Randolph, of Roanoke, when excited, would sometimes inadvertently use the name of the Almighty irreverently; but, like that great orator, he would feel deep humility for it afterwards. This erratic nature was only a flimsy cloak which hid one of the most large-hearted, generous, and tender dispositions that could be found. Though stern and unyielding in the heat of argument, yet the next moment he would exhibit the tender, sympathetic feeling of a generous, loving heart. His care and affection for his slaves were intense. Hearing of the arrest and imprisonment of a favorite negro boy, under suspicion of robbery, though late at night, and during a blinding snow-storm, he rode to the jail, a distance of ten miles, and by his efforts had him acquitted. Upon reaching home with the lad behind him, the whole family, white and black, met him to know the result; but Mr. Meriwether, with pent-up feelings of rejoicing, could only murmur, "Acquitted," and then both master and mistress, with all their blacks, burst into tears for joy. Here was a scene for the anti-slavery screechers. Mr. Meriwether was a firm believer in mesmerism, and his experiments in this mysterious art were the subject of much wonder and superstition, especially among the negroes, who would declare that "Mars Peter would mes'rize 'em," which greatly served to keep them in strict obedience. But his neighbors and friends laughed at the theory and would not be convinced. Mr. Meriwether, however, determined to make a practical test of the new science, and prove to his sceptical friends that he was right. So, calling from the field, one day, a negro boy of fifteen years named Willis (who was perfectly ignorant of his master's intentions), he then made a private experiment in putting him under the mesmeric influence, and, to his great delight, quickly succeeded in having him under complete control. Being now fully convinced of the success of his theory, he invited his friends and neighbors to witness a performance in this mysterious art. The excitement and novelty of such a wonderful exhibition served to draw quite a large number of the more scientific and learned neighbors, among whom were Mr. and

SOUTH-WEST MOUNTAINS

Mrs. William C. Rives, the grandparents of the authoress Amélie Rives, Dr. Thomas Meriwether, Mr. Francis K. Nelson, Mr. James Terrell, the Rev. E. Boyden, and many others.

It did not take long for Mr. Meriwether to put the boy Willis under his influence, who followed his master into the crowded parlor with closed eyes, seeming oblivious to all present. After being securely blindfolded, so as to prevent any possible deception, a number of interesting experiments were made to test the truth of his somnambulistic actions. First, Mrs. Rives brought forth several colored balls of worsted upon a waiter; Mr. Meriwether touched one of the balls, which were held behind his back, Willis at once told the color of the ball that was touched; a number of glasses of water were then brought in, one of which Mr. Meriwether tasted, the boy, after tasting each one, told the right one; a number of handkerchiefs from the company were thrown together, among which was Mr. Meriwether's; after being well mixed and rolled together, Willis quickly undid the parcel and produced his master's handkerchief by smelling each one; Mr. Meriwether then tasted some sugar, pepper, and salt, and in each case Willis told what he tasted; when the pepper was tasted Willis began to spit and make a wry face, saying something burnt his tongue, though he had not touched the pepper. He was now told to bring his mistress from another room; this he did, pulling her along with some force. He was then told to *kiss* his mistress; this he also attempted to do, much to the merriment of the company, until he was commanded to desist. He was then made to assume various positions, which his master would make behind his back. No one had any control of him except Mr. Meriwether, and he would not obey even his mistress, to whom he was always faithful and obedient; it was thus conclusively proved that the boy Willis was entirely controlled by the will of his master, and was entirely unconscious of his own actions. At another time, Mr. Meriwether put a servant-girl of one of his neighbors under the mesmeric influence; but in this case the girl could not be awakened afterwards, but continued to sleep for many days. It was found that she had concealed a tin box of trinkets in her bosom, which was considered the cause of this curious case. Mr. Meriwether would frequently mesmerize the hand of a young person, so that it could not be removed from a table. We give these experiments, as made by Mr. Meriwether in 1847, with the belief that they were the first in mesmerism ever successfully performed in Virginia. The boy Willis, now an old man, is still living in Charlottesville, and there are many persons who were witness to their performance who can also testify to them.

Mr. Meriwether was a most judicious and successful farmer. He studied the old *Farmers' Register* of 1835 very closely, and was a firm disciple of that father of agriculture, Edmund Ruffin. The Cismont farm was very rich, much of it having been but recently cleared of the

SOUTH-WEST MOUNTAINS

original forests, and from the virgin soil teeming crops of corn, wheat, and tobacco would be produced. Such was the quantity of hay that in 1841 Mr. Meriwether delivered annually for several years more than twenty-five tons each year to the stage yards. A Northern gentleman about this time visited the farm, and, after viewing the droves of fat sheep and cattle, the sleek horses, the well-fed, happy negroes, and the great abundance on every hand, turned to Mr. Meriwether and said, "How is it, sir, that everything I see on your place is fat except yourself?"

"Well, sir," replied Mr. Meriwether, "you will see my *better* half at the house." Mr. Meriwether was noted for being quite thin and his wife quite stout.

It was also at this time that Miss Julia Willis, the sister of the celebrated author and poet N. P. Willis, of Boston, visited the place, bringing with her the prejudices of New England against negro slavery. She rode over the beautiful fields, saw the peaceful, contented slaves at their labor, swinging the cradle through the golden grain to the merry song and chorus of the reapers; viewed their comfortable houses and the humane treatment by both master and mistress; and then she wrote her people that "the slaves of Virginia were so only in name, and seemed more free and happy than many in New England."

In 1847 the house was greatly enlarged and improved by the addition of a rear wing. This made it more commodious; but even with this enlargement it could scarcely accommodate the host of friends who continued to visit this home of magnificent hospitalities. The chief attraction here was the gentle, loving mistress. She was always the "good Samaritan," and responded to every appeal; to her would go both young and old, rich and poor, who would pour into her sympathetic heart their love-scrapes, their troubles, their joys and sorrows, and "Cousin Fanny" was sure to solve each difficulty and bring the sunshine into every heart.

During the exciting war period Cismont was frequently the scene of martial display. Here General James L. Kemper, the hero of Gettysburg, with his aides, would visit his family, who were here as refugees, and over the green lawn would bivouac his men; or it would resound to the tramp and bugle-blast of the "Albemarle Light-Horse" cavalry when drilled by its gallant first lieutenant, George H. Geiger.

Both Mr. and Mrs. Meriwether died from home, Mr. Meriwether in 1850 at the Hot Springs, Virginia, and Mrs. Meriwether in 1883 at Clover Fields, the adjoining farm, in her eighty-fifth year. Cismont then passed into the possession of George G. Randolph, a descendant of the Meriwether family. After his death it was bought, in 1894, by its present owner, Colonel H. W. Fuller, of the Chesapeake and Ohio Railroad, who obtained the mansion and four hundred acres surrounding it.

Upon taking possession of this old homestead,

SOUTH-WEST MOUNTAINS

Colonel Fuller at once began its transformation into the beautiful modern structure which it now presents, and with that energy and executive ability which so characterize him, has changed the hills and dales and all the surroundings of old Cismont into visions of beauty and attractiveness, which at once arrests the traveller as it breaks into view from the public road.

The cut which is given presents the building as it now appears, with its lofty columns, double porticos, and massive chimneys, which loom above the tree-tops, giving it quite a castellated appearance. The approach to the mansion is by a winding roadway through verdant fields and over rustic stone bridges, until, entering the widespread lawn of ten acres, dotted with stately oaks, elms, and forest-trees, and enriched on all sides by highly-colored flowers and tropical plants, one feels that here is presented one of the most picturesque and idealistic spots, such as the combination of nature and art can alone create into a truly elysian home.

One of the most unique and interesting objects at Cismont is the old kitchen, which is seen on the left; this building has a history in itself, and is now transformed into a museum of Colonial relics and souvenirs of the late war. The building once stood on the mountain-side, but at the erection of the new mansion it was moved by Mr. Meriwether in 1835, and used as a kitchen, placing it about fifty feet from the house, as was customary in those days in always having the kitchen apart from the main dwelling. On one side was built a shed-room as sleeping apartment for the cook, while on the other side was a similar room, which was occupied at one time by a poor white woman named Miss Lucy Duke, who came from Louisa County, and was employed by Mr. Meriwether as housekeeper until her death. She was supposed to be very poor, without friends, relatives, or means to support her; but after her death it was found that she had six hundred dollars laid away in her little room. Immediately there sprang up many relatives to mourn her death and claim the money, but by her will she gave it all to Mr. Meriwether, who had befriended her for so many years.

The old kitchen is preserved in the same primitive style as of Colonial times, with its rough-hewn timbers and wrought nails. Here is seen the wide hearth with its deep jambs and long crane, where all the meals were cooked for the plantation; large logs of wood, four feet long, would be piled upon its immense andirons, upon which would be spread many ovens and kettles, while its large hearth would be covered with huge ash-cakes, to be baked on the hot bricks.

"Aunt Nancy" was the presiding genius here, who held complete sway over this department, much to the terror of the young darkies; but the writer can well remember her kind and generous heart, as being the recipient of many a good meal upon the old hearth. The room with its cupboards and shelves is now adorned with many relics,—Indian pipes, old swords, knives and forks,

THE OLD COLONIAL KITCHEN AT CISMONT

candlesticks, bits, keys, and bridles, all of a past age; its furniture of antique chairs and tables date nearly a hundred years; its walls are adorned with pictures of battle-fields and scenes along the Chesapeake and Ohio Railway, while huge Chinese lanterns and Japanese ware adorn the upper loft. Altogether, the old kitchen presents an inviting aspect, over the door of which is its motto, "Sans cérémonie." Here the pipe of peace can be smoked in luxuriant ease and abandon, with a drink of cider from the cupboard, or a draught of "malt and hops, which beat pills and drops," or, if to be preferred, "ash-cake and buttermilk," as in ye olden time.

Here the colonel surrounds himself with his genial friends and entertains them with war stories or exciting railroad scenes, until the young blood boils with enthusiasm and breaks forth in merry song.

Colonel H. W. Fuller is the son of David Fuller, of Massachusetts; he was so named for his two uncles. David Fuller was a descendant of John Fuller, who is said to have emigrated to America in 1635, coming over with John Winthrop in the ship "Abigail," Hackwell, master, and settled in Cambridge village (now Newton) in 1644. From him sprang all the Fullers in this country. They were a bold, hardy set of men, persevering and energetic under difficulties, and these traits are still shown in their descendants.

Colonel Fuller enlisted in the late war when quite young (only sixteen) and served with distinction during the four years. He commanded at first a company in one of the New York regiments and rose rapidly to the rank of colonel. He still preserves his well-worn sword upon many a hard-fought battle-field, and can relate some thrilling adventures. After the war Colonel Fuller came South and identified himself with the Chesapeake and Ohio Railroad, since which time he has taken great interest in this Piedmont section and other parts of the State through which the road traverses, investing largely in its lands, and aiding in the development of the mineral and agricultural interests of the State. Colonel Fuller married Cora Johnson, the daughter of Thomas Johnson, Esq., of Virginia, who is of the same family as Senator Johnston, of Virginia, though the t in the name has been dropped.

Two daughters have graced this beautiful home. The eldest, Nellie, married Mr. Talbot, of Louisville, Kentucky, but now of Washington City. The youngest, Lucille, with graceful form and sparkling eye, sheds a beam of radiant joy at the old homestead, filling its halls with mirth and music as of old.

CLOVER FIELDS
The Old Home of the Meriwethers. Now owned by Frank M. Randolph, Esq.

CLOVER FIELDS

THE OLD HOME OF THE MERIWETHERS

BEYOND all doubt Clover Fields, the present country-seat of Mr. Frank M. Randolph, which comes next to Cismont, is the oldest settlement along the South-West Mountains, and one of the few farms still held by the descendants of Colonel Nicholas Meriwether of Colonial fame, who by cunning craft so ingratiated himself into the good graces of his majesty George II. as to obtain his large grant of land, which embraced most of this beautiful section of Albemarle. As has been previously observed in our notice of Cismont, the Meriwethers are reported to be of Quaker origin, but we have reason to believe that these were but a small portion of the wide-spread English Meriwethers, who were chiefly of the Established Church, as we read of the Rev. Francis Meriwether, of Somerset County, who died in 1806, and of the Rev. J. Meriwether, who was chaplain to the Duchess of Clarence in 1824.

From old records we gather that Nicholas Meriwether, the first of the family, was born in Wales, and died in England in 1678. It is doubted whether he ever came to America, though tradition says he obtained a large grant of land from

Charles II. He had five sons, only three of whom, Nicholas, Francis, and David, are known to have come to America very early in its settlement. Of these three we will only regard more particularly the eldest, Nicholas (2d), as from him courses the Meriwether blood in nearly every prominent family of Virginia, either directly or by intermarriage.

This Nicholas (2d) is supposed to have come over previous to the year 1685, as Bishop Meade, in his "Old Churches," speaks of him as a vestryman at St. Peter's Church, New Kent County, in that year. This is the Nicholas Meriwether who obtained his large grant of seventeen thousand nine hundred and fifty-two acres in 1730 from George II., which embraced all the lands lying along the South-West Mountains. This patent was signed by William Gooch, then governor of the colony, and is still preserved. This "Colonel" Nicholas (2d) married a Miss Crawford, daughter of David Crawford, Esq., of Assasquin, New Kent County, in 1744, and had nine children. The eldest, Jane, married Colonel Robert Lewis, of Belvoir, Albemarle County. This branch, which embraces most of the Lewis family, we will speak of more fully hereafter. The fifth son, David, married Anne Holmes, daughter of George Holmes, Esq., of King and Queen County, Virginia, and settled in Louisa County, inheriting a portion of his father's large estate. He died there December 25, 1744, and his wife died March 11, 1735. They had eight

SOUTH-WEST MOUNTAINS

children. The eldest, Thomas Meriwether, married Elizabeth Thornton. They had eleven children,—four sons and seven daughters.

Nicholas Meriwether, the eldest son of Nicholas (2d), was born in 1736, and married Margaret Douglas, only daughter of the Rev. William Douglas, of Louisa County, Virginia. This Nicholas, third in descent from the first Nicholas, inherited the most of his father's property in Albemarle, and after his marriage, in 1760, with Margaret Douglas moved to the county, and settled at Clover Fields, building there one of the first houses erected along the mountains, the house at Castle Hill being also built about the same time.

Here "Colonel Nick" Meriwether and Margaret Douglas lived and raised a family of six children; first, William Douglas, who married Elizabeth Lewis in 1788 (she was the daughter of Nicholas Lewis and Mary Walker); he was always called "Captain Billy" and his wife "Aunt Betsy." They inherited, lived, and died at Clover Fields. The other sons of "Colonel Nick" were Thomas, who married Anne Minor, daughter of Garret Minor, of Louisa County. He lived with his grandfather, "Parson" Douglas, and became a most successful farmer. Nicholas Hunter married Rebecca Terrell. Charles married, first, Lydia Laurie; second, Nancy Minor; and, third, Mary D. Walton. Francis married Catherine Davis. Elizabeth, their only daughter, married Thomas Walker Lewis.

"Captain Billy" and Elizabeth Lewis had seven

children. The first two died young; his third son, William Hunter, commonly called "Billy Fish," married Frances Poindexter, and lived some time at the present Castalia farm, which was then a part of the Meriwether tract. It is said that this "Billy Fish" had a great penchant for building mills. He built one at Clover Fields, the site of which is yet seen, also one which was located near the present woollen-mills near Charlottesville; he also built the first bridge across the Rivanna, where the railroad now crosses it, which was called "Meriwether's Bridge"; but late in life he either traded or sold all of his mills and property in Virginia and moved to Texas, where he built more mills.

The third son and seventh child of "Captain Billy" was Dr. Thomas Walker Meriwether, who was born in 1803 at Clover Fields, and died there in 1863. He married Anne Carter Nelson, and located at Kinloch, as we shall further note. Of the two daughters of "Captain Billy," Margaret Douglas (who was always called "Cousin Peggy") married, first, her cousin, Dr. Frank Thornton Meriwether, and second, Francis Kinlaw Nelson, by whom no issue. Of her first marriage were two children,—Charles James, who married his cousin and settled in Bedford County, and Mary Walker Meriwether, who married Major Thomas Jefferson Randolph, eldest son of Colonel Thomas Jefferson Randolph, of Edgehill. Their children were Frank Meriwether Randolph, who married Charlotte N. Macon, Thomas Jefferson,

THE FIRST CLOVER FIELDS MANSION
Built 1760

SOUTH-WEST MOUNTAINS

Margaret Douglas, Francis Nelson, and George Geiger.

After the death of Mrs. Margaret Douglas Nelson the Clover Fields estate went to her grandson, Frank M. Randolph, and his children, who now reside there, the ninth generation in descent from the first Nicholas Meriwether.

The second daughter of "Captain Billy" and Elizabeth Lewis—Mary Walker, who was called "Polly"—married her cousin, Peter M. Meriwether, and lived at Cismont, as we have already shown

We have now traced the family possession to, and will speak more fully of, the history past and present of this celebrated old homestead.

We give a picture of the old mansion which sheltered so many generations of the sons and daughters of this truly great and extended family. It is vividly impressed on the memory of the writer as it looked in 1845, presenting the same peculiar types of architecture so often found belonging to the period 1700, with its long, low porch in front, from the eaves of which rose a high, peaked roof, set off with small dormer-windows for its many narrow rooms above. Immense tall chimneys towered above the tree-tops, around whose wide hearths had gathered many generations at happy reunions. The many out-buildings surrounding the mansion—kitchen, meat-house, dairy, stables, barns, mills, and numerous negro cabins—gave it the appearance of quite a village, which would be still further heightened by droves of horses, vehicles, and troops of negroes passing to and fro. Here in the long porch "Colonel Nick" would sit and entertain his numerous friends with his experience in the "Braddock war," and how he, with three others, bore the wounded and defeated general from the battle-field; and then would point with pride to the gold-laced embroidered coat sent him from Ireland by Braddock's sister, which for a long time hung in the Clover Fields parlor as a war relic; and then "Aunt Peggy" would tell of her Scotch kindred, her home in the Old World, her youthful recollections of the voyage to America, and the exciting times of the Revolution. She would always have gathered around her troops of old and young to listen eagerly to these truthful stories. After this noble, kind-hearted couple passed away, being the last connecting link between the "Colonial" and the "new nation," their places were taken by "Captain Billy" and "Aunt Betsy." He would sit in the same seat and tell of the war of 1812, while she with delight related anecdotes of her "Lewis" and "Walker" kin, whose prowess during that exciting war period has become a part of history. It is said that Clover Fields could show more old china, old furniture, old books, and other Colonial relics than any other place along the mountains; many of these had been brought direct from England and Scotland by the Rev. William Douglas, the grandfather of "Captain Billy," whose large and valuable library was once at Clover Fields, but which has since been scattered among his numerous descendants. "Aunt Betsy" would always with pride bring forth these family heirlooms and give their history, which would now be of priceless value to the antiquarian.

"Colonel Nick" Meriwether was quite active and prominent in the church, being mentioned by Bishop Meade as a vestryman in 1762, in connection with Thomas Jefferson, Dr. George Gilmer, and others in the establishment of old Walker's Church. His son, William D. Meriwether, was also added to the vestry in 1787. It was at this time that he and Mr. Jefferson were ordered by the vestry "to lay off two acres of land, including a space around Walker's Church," land which had been given to the parish by John Walker, of Belvoir. This makes us suppose that Captain William Meriwether was, like Jefferson, a skilled surveyor. This fact is also made more probable by an old copy of Gibson's "Surveying" of 1803, now in the hands of the writer, in which are the names of "Nicholas L. Meriwether, William and Mary College, 1809," and "Charles J. Meriwether, 1816," both of whom were sons of Captain William D. Meriwether, who used it. Thus it is presumed they all inherited a love for this science. Nicholas L., it is believed, died early. Charles J. Meriwether, his younger brother, outlived them all, and is still fresh in the remembrance of many now living. He bore strikingly the Meriwether characteristics of a generous, kind-hearted temperament, but with always decided opinions of his own upon every topic. He it was who came out upon the portico at Clover Fields, one day, during the civil war, as the "Yankees" rode up, and greeted them in his usual urbane and genial manner, thinking they were Confederate officers; nor did he find out his mistake until they had relieved him of his handsome gold watch and threatened to make him a prisoner.

The old book of surveying mentioned had also the name of Thomas Lewis Meriwether, who was one of the sons of Thomas Meriwether and Anne Minor, of Louisa County, and who died in 1838, unmarried. The old book, from its well worn appearance, must have been often handled by Jefferson, Meriwether Lewis, and other noted surveyors of the time who visited "Captain Billy."

Clover Fields, even at a very early period, became the rendezvous for the clergy, laity, professional, and political men of the day, besides a vast kindred from all sections. No one bearing the name of Meriwether, Walker, or Lewis, or being of the most remote kin, could pass Clover Fields without a visit to "Captain Billy" and "Aunt Betsy," and partake of their bounteous hospitality; even the stranger and wayfaring pilgrim were welcomed, so that the old house was always filled with guests, who would often spend weeks at a time with them.

After the death of William Douglas Meriwether and his wife, in 1845, the Clover Fields estate descended to his second daughter, Margaret Douglas Meriwether, who, with her second husband, Francis K. Nelson, lived and died there. It was about

SOUTH-WEST MOUNTAINS

the year 1846 that the old Colonial house was removed to give place to the present modern structure, which was erected by Mr. Nelson, whose taste and culture were far in advance of his day.

This spacious mansion, at the time of its completion, exceeded any in the neighborhood for beauty and utility. Here, in more modern style, the hospitalities continued to be dispensed with a liberal hand, and "Cousin Peggy," like her great-grandmother, bestowed blessings upon all around her, such as never will be forgotten by those who were the fortunate recipients. Mr. Nelson was a most striking man, and one long to be remembered; with a *suaviter in modo et fortiter in re*, combined with an exactness and neatness which were always shown, not only in person, but enforced in the more minute details of the farm, bearing always a pleasant, cheerful temperament, with fine conversational powers, he made Clover Fields very attractive, and sustained the traditional hospitality of his forefathers in an eminent degree.

The Clover Fields farm has always been noted for its fertility and productiveness; its waving fields of clover, from which it derives its name; its bounteous crops of wheat and tobacco, the latter of which was mostly sent to England; its celebrated garden, which always bore the earliest vegetables in the neighborhood; its lofty cherry-trees, from which many an urchin fell in his eager grasp for the luscious fruit; its immense crop of apples; its droves of fat sheep and cattle, like those of the celebrated Robert Blakewell, of England, which were too dear for any one to purchase and too fat for any one to eat,—all these have rendered it famous, and won for it years ago the *sobriquet* of "Model Farm."

One of the most interesting spots at Clover Fields is the family burying-lot, in one corner of the garden. Here on its many moss-covered tombstones can be read the names of most of the Meriwethers who have lived and died at this old place, dating back into the past century. Here sleep undisturbed on their native ground those noble men and women who lived in the exciting times of the Revolution and saw the wild country emerge into a "new nation," and, with hearts glowing with love and patriotism, gently sank to rest, beloved by all around them. Here are also gathered families and connections, and even many strangers who have sickened and died within the walls of the old house, until the little cemetery is completely filled. It is now kept sacred, and forms a valuable guide-post to the historian in his search for the early characters in Virginia's history.

Of late years Clover Fields has become a pleasant resort each summer for those who seek its cool mountain breezes, or love to roam over its picturesque hills and dales or secluded woodland retreats. Here one can tread the same spot where the wild Indian once made his tenting-ground, or can view the same landscape which broke upon the first settlers of Albemarle, and feel that he is indeed upon historic ground.

CASTALIA
The Home of the Lewises. Now owned by Murray Bocock, Esq.

CASTALIA

THE ESTATE OF MURRAY BOOCOCK, ESQ.

LEWIS! How the name thrills the heart with patriotic emotions! What scenes of valor and deeds of daring does it recall as, like a brilliant picture, it speaks of the heroes of the past!

Next to that of Washington there is no name which stands forth more prominently upon the page of Virginia history than that of Lewis. Even from the first settlement of the infant colony we have General Robert Lewis, who landed on the shores of Virginia in 1600; then Colonel John Lewis, of His Majesty's Council; after whom came General Andrew Lewis, the bold frontier warrior, whose noble statue stands close to that of Washington at Richmond, Virginia; and then Robert Lewis, the intimate friend and secretary of Washington; and Colonel Fielding Lewis, who married the sister of Washington; and Meriwether Lewis, the explorer of the West; and many of the name who have graced our legislative halls even to the present day, all attest the fact that the name is the symbol for all that is noble, brave, and chivalrous.

Before entering upon Castalia, a short genealogical sketch of the family may not be inappropriate.

General Robert Lewis, the first of the family, was the son of Sir Edward Lewis, of Beacon, Wales, and was said to be descended from the Duke of Dorset. This first Robert Lewis received a grant from the Crown for thirty-three thousand three hundred and thirty-three and one-third acres of land in Gloucester County, Virginia, where he first located and built his celebrated mansion, Warner Hall, descriptions of which sound more like the baronial castles of England than the primitive dwellings of the colonists. It is here that he lived in such regal style. All the furnishings of the house and even luxuries for the table were wafted up the York River from across the Atlantic, that he might keep up the princely living as of the landed gentry in the mother country.

John Lewis, the eldest son of Robert, was sent to England to be educated, and while there married Isabella Warner, a great heiress and sister of the famous Speaker Warner, of Virginia.

This son John (1st) had also a son named John (2d), who married Elizabeth, the youngest daughter of Speaker Warner. Their son John (3d) married Frances Fielding, and inherited Warner Hall, with all its silver plate, pictures, and jewels.

John (2d) and Elizabeth Warner had a son, Robert, who married Jane Meriwether, the daughter of Colonel Nicholas Meriwether, who obtained his large grant in Albemarle in 1730. This Robert, who was a colonel in the Revolutionary war, after his marriage moved and settled at Belvoir, in Albemarle, being a part of his father-in-law's large estate. Colonel Robert Lewis had a son, Nicholas, who married Mary Walker, the daughter of Dr. Thomas Walker, of Castle Hill; they lived on a fine plantation near Charlottesville, Virginia, called The Farm, which we shall note hereafter. Their son, Thomas Walker Lewis, married Elizabeth Meriwether, sister of "Captain Billy" Meriwether, of Clover Fields. They lived at Locust Grove, which was a part of The Farm; it was here that their son, Robert W. Lewis, was born in 1808. This Robert (who was second cousin of Captain Robert Lewis, Washington's secretary) afterwards became the owner of Castalia, but only by purchase rather than by inheritance, to which he was entitled through his mother, who was the daughter of Colonel Nicholas Meriwether and Margaret Douglas, of Clover Fields.

The Castalia farm, lying between Clover Fields and Belvoir, containing about one thousand acres, was a part of the Meriwether grant gained by the first Nicholas Meriwether in 1730, during the reign of George II., the patent being signed by William Gooch, then governor of the colony. Warner Lewis, of Warner Hall, a nephew of Colonel Robert Lewis, of Belvoir, had already married the daughter-in-law of Governor Gooch, and doubtless was influential in gaining this large grant.

To what limits this large body of land extended over the county is not known, though it must have embraced most of its entire area. Think of these two landed nabobs—Colonel Robert Lewis, with his thirty-three thousand three hundred and thirty-three and one-third acres, and Colonel Nicholas (2d) Meriwether, with nearly twenty thousand acres—owning almost two counties of Virginia!

The first to live at Castalia is said to have been an old negro named "Jack," whose cabin stood near the present spring from which flows a bold stream through the plantation, which is still known as "Jack's Branch."

The first habitable building of any size was built in 1747 by "Colonel Nick" Meriwether before going to Clover Fields. This was only a double log cabin, perched near the old spring, and surrounded by a grove of oaks; it is still standing, showing a wonderful state of preservation. "Captain Billy" Meriwether, who inherited all of these lands, gave Castalia to his son, William Hunter, known as "Billy Fish," who married Miss Poindexter. He lived in the old log cabin for some time, adding to it the framed part at the rear, and was the first to give it the classical name of Castalia, for the celebrated mythological fountain on Mount Parnassus, sacred to Apollo and the Muses, of which "Billy" imagined his spring at the foot of the mountain to be typical.

After the death of "Billy Fish," his widow sold the farm to John H. Craven, of Pen Park, who gave it afterwards to his son William somewhere in the thirties. Robert W. Lewis, of Locust Grove, had married Sally Craven, daughter of the late P. H. Craven. They continued to live there until 1833, when he moved to his patrimony, Piedmont, across the river, the present farm of Mr. Triplett Haxall, who bought it of the late Richard O'Mohundro.

After living there for thirteen years, Mr. Lewis exchanged the farm for Castalia, giving William Craven three thousand dollars to boot. Thus we see how the Castalia farm again came into the possession of the Lewises.

For a number of years Mr. Lewis occupied the old log cabin, which had been just previous to his taking possession rented by Mr. Peter Cobbs, the father of the present Mrs. John C. Patterson, of Charlottesville. This good old gentleman had many peculiarities, one of which was always wearing his hat in the house. He had once been a teacher, and was fond of asking young people intricate questions upon their studies, which would often puzzle children of a larger growth.

In 1850, Mr. Lewis erected the present commodious building which adorns the neighborhood. At that time the forests had remained almost untouched of their original growth, and it is said that Mr. Lewis marked each tree to be used for his house, picking only the finest and best. It was a little before the days of planing-mills, so each piece had to be dressed by hand, which was slow and tedious; the brick were made upon the spot by his own slaves, and within a year's time there arose the present large structure, a monument to his skill and careful supervision.

In 1853, Mr. Lewis opened a small school, more particularly for the education of his own children. For this purpose he employed a most accomplished English lady. The school was limited to ten, but more than that number of happy, joyous girls usually filled the house, making it a scene of constant fun and frolic. "Cousin Sally Bob," as she was always called, was ever ready to enter into the frolics of the girls and see that they had a "good time." The young bloods of the neighborhood would therefore always be encouraged, and would often make night hideous with banjo and fiddle in their serenades, which would be sure to end in an invitation to a big supper and a dance with the girls.

On one occasion one of these gallants (now a dignified alderman) wished to play a quiet game of chess with the captive of his heart while the family were away, hoping thereby to make a conquest. "Cousin Sally," who was in the scheme, cautioned her "old man Bob" to leave the young couple to themselves, while she took the rest of the girls to a party; but Mr. Lewis became so interested in the game that he forgot the admonition, and was a close observer the entire evening, thereby preventing what might have been a union of hearts and hands.

Such were the attractions of Castalia that it was styled the "Home of the Graces"; but its happy band of girls was soon after scattered, each to grace a home of her own.

SOUTH-WEST MOUNTAINS

On the 25th of May, 1877, the head of this happy home died, and was buried beside his beloved wife, in the rear of the old log cabin where they had lived so long humbly and contentedly.

Robert W. Lewis was no ordinary man. Few could fail to be impressed by his tall, erect figure, his open and benevolent countenance, his warm grasp of the hand, and hearty voice as he welcomed all who honored him with a visit. He exhibited in a striking degree the Lewis traits, true republican simplicity, natural and unassumed; his dress of plain homespun, his extreme love of truth and honesty, causing him to abhor all shams or pretence. Being reticent and slow of speech, he retired from all argument or political strife, and yet ever ready to give a clear and decided opinion on every topic when the occasion required. His powerful frame and great courage often made him a terror to evil-doers around him. On one occasion, while at Piedmont, his father-in-law had a quantity of grain stolen by some boatmen from Milton; learning that these men, who were powerfully-built fellows, had the wheat on their boat and were leaving for Richmond, Mr. Lewis at once gave chase, overtook the boat, boarded it by some ruse, where he found the wheat, which they could not account for; he then single-handed pitched the men overboard and brought the boat back to Pen Park.

Such is an imperfect sketch of this true Virginia gentleman, whose many sterling qualities made him a fit representative of the noble family of Lewis.

Of his sons and daughters, George, the eldest, was accidentally killed while hunting, May 22, 1855. Robert Walker married Elizabeth, daughter of Dr. James Minor, of Music Hall, and lives in Richmond. Thomas Walker married Jane, daughter of Frederick W. Page, librarian of the University of Virginia, and lives on a portion of Castalia farm. John married Miss Austin, and lives in Albemarle. Elizabeth married Mr. John Hamilton, of Charlottesville, Virginia. Alice married her cousin, James T. Lewis, who mounted his horse and joined the Confederate army an hour after the ceremony was performed, in 1861; they are both dead. Ellen married A. J. Smith, who lives in Fauquier County, Virginia. Margaret married Eugene Sampson; and Lydia, the youngest, married Henry Lewis Smith, of Smithfield, West Virginia.

In 1881 Castalia was sold to Mr. Bartlett Bolling, of Petersburg, Virginia, who made many improvements which added greatly to its appearance. In the spring of 1894 it was sold to Mr. Murray Boocock, of New York City, its present owner.

This gentleman, having travelled over Europe as well as this country, was attracted, while passing through the Southern States, by this beautiful section of Virginia, as possessing more advantages than any he had met with in the South. Here he found among these picturesque hills a fertile soil, a genial atmosphere, and a refined people, the descendants of a once proud and noble aristocracy.

SOUTH-WEST MOUNTAINS

Castalia has fallen into no mean hands, but, like those who once occupied it, can also boast of a lineage that touches the Georges of England, and whose patriotic ancestry have marched to the slogan of '76.

Mr. Boocock is the son of Samuel Ward Boocock, Esq., who has long been one of the prominent residents of Brooklyn, living on its historic Heights. He is connected with many of the leading institutions of Brooklyn, and also occupies a foremost position among the bankers of New York. Mr. Samuel W. Boocock married Mary C. Underhill, the daughter of Elias Underhill, who married Jane C. Carpenter. Mr. Murray Boocock is therefore descended on his maternal side from one of the most illustrious families in this country. We find in 1416 that Captain John Underhill, commonly called Lord Underhill, and Agnes, his wife, were seated at Cunningham in Warwickshire, and in 1587 occurs the name of Sir Hercules Underhill, Knight and High Sheriff of the County. The noted Edward Underhill, one of Queen Mary's band of gentlemen pensioners in 1558, was also a member of the family. Captain John Underhill was a distinguished officer in the British army, who had served with great distinction in Ireland and Cadiz. He emigrated to America in 1632 and settled at Kenelworth, Oyster Bay, Long Island. Much of interest concerning this Captain John Underhill, who was very prominent in the early history of New England and New York, could be given did space permit. An account of his many exploits and other interesting information can be found in a volume called the "Algerine Captive," from the pen of a descendant, John Underhill, of New York.

Nathaniel Underhill, the younger son of Captain John, moved to Westchester, and bought lands of John Turner in 1687. He married Mary Ferris, a descendant of the great Ferris family of Leicestershire, England, who are said to have obtained large grants of land from William the Conqueror. Their son Abraham married Hannah Cromwell, and their son Abraham (2d) married, first, Phœbe Hallock, and second, Kesiah Farrington. The son of this second marriage, Solomon Underhill, of Sing Sing, married Phœbe Concklin, and their son Townsend married Emily Smith. He died in 1817, leaving one son, Elias Underhill, who married Jane C. Carpenter; these two are the grandparents of Mr. Murray Boocock, of Castalia. A great shadow fell upon the community of Brooklyn Heights, May, 1896, by the death of Mrs. Samuel Ward Boocock. She was one of the most esteemed and charming women who figured in its social life. Mrs. Boocock was admired and esteemed by all who knew her for her great tact, kindliness, and unobtrusive generosity. She was always active in charitable and philanthropic enterprises, and will be greatly missed by all with whom she was associated.

In the spring of 1894, Mr. Boocock married Miss Ada Miriam Dike, daughter of the late Camden C. Dike, of Brooklyn. Mr. Dike was

SOUTH-WEST MOUNTAINS

born in Providence, Rhode Island, September 18, 1832, and died quite suddenly of pneumonia, October 11, 1894, at Point Pleasant, New Jersey. For thirty-six years he was engaged in the wool business under the firm of " Dike Brothers." He was also quite prominent in the business circles of New York and Brooklyn, being trustee for South Brooklyn Savings Bank and other institutions. He was also a member of the Chamber of Commerce, and president of the Apollo Club.

Mr. Dike married Miss Jennie Staunton Scott, granddaughter of Major-General Phineas Staunton, who was so prominent in the war of 1812. She is also closely connected with the family of General Winfield Scott, Colonel John Scott of the Confederate war being also a near relative.

Mr. and Mrs. Dike also lived on the beautiful Heights of Brooklyn, so long noted for its handsome residences and refined, cultivated society, composed as it is of many of the oldest families in the State.

Let us now glance at the new Castalia, seated at the foot of the Albemarle " Mount Parnassus," near the clear Castalian spring, which still sends forth its invigorating waters as of old, changing those who partake of them into modern *Castalides*, since those who have here dwelt have always exhibited the poetry of thought and motion.

The top of the stately mansion can scarcely be seen from the entrance to the grounds, nearly a mile distant; but as we reach a commanding summit it breaks upon the view in all its grandeur and beauty. Seated amid a dense grove of trees, its balustrades and lofty chimneys tower above the tree-tops, while through the dense foliage can be seen its many windows and tall columns of the portico. The picture is still more heightened by an expansive lawn, with luxuriant orchards and gardens on each side, while in the background rises the majestic mountain, which gives to the whole a grand and impressive scene.

As we enter this handsome home of English type we are at once removed a century in time. To one side of the spacious hall stands a " grandfather's" clock, whose sonorous tones give a saddened pleasure as it marks the flight of time. The walls, like those of the baronets, are adorned with trophies of the chase, one of which is a fine specimen of the head and antlers of a caribou or moose deer of Maine, which is now nearly extinct. Sketches in nature also adorn its walls, while stately palms and towering plants make it a veritable *salle de verdure*. Turning to the drawing-room, we enter truly a *salon d'art*, where one can feast the eye. Here are choice scenes from Shakespeare by the celebrated John and Josiah Boydell, as found in the Shakespearian Gallery at Pall Mall, 1793. This John Boydell was famous in the graphic art. He was lord mayor of London, and died in 1804. Mr. Boocock has the only two of his works now in this country. Two fine engravings printed on satin, the " King's Favorite" and " Rubens the Artist," from the Vanderbilt collection in New York, are also worthy of admiration.

HERD OF HEREFORDS AT CASTALIA FARM

SOUTH-WEST MOUNTAINS

An exquisite oil-painting upon silk tapestry from Paris of Bougereau's "Cupid and Psyche"; a fine engraving on wood is shown of the "Dying Lion," being an exact copy as cut in the solid rock at Geneva. Many other delicate etchings are among this rare collection, which Mr. Boocock has secured at great expense. Then the many curios and *bric-à-brac* from foreign lands will captivate the visitor; but the most to be admired is a solid silver flagon, eighteen inches high, having rich carvings of Indian scenery. This was one of the exhibits at the Columbian Exposition at Chicago, 1893, sent from India. It was presented to Mr. and Mrs. Boocock as a wedding-present.

The entire Castalia mansion is furnished in antique oak of the past century, and each of its many bedrooms are in a different color, with draperies and curtains to match. Hot and cold water is conveyed over the whole house from an immense tank in the roof; and beside its many fireplaces, it is heated also by a furnace below. It is difficult to conceive of a more complete and elegant country residence, one such, indeed, as would fittingly adorn any city.

Of late, Mr. Boocock has turned his attention to the development of a higher grade of cattle in Virginia; for this purpose he has imported a thoroughbred Hereford bull, Salisbury, from the herd of John Price, Court-House, Pembridge, England, at a cost of three thousand dollars, together with his mate, Curly Lady, besides several cows of the same breed. These have recently taken the champion winnings at the State fairs of New Jersey, Ohio, West Virginia, and Maryland. Mr. Boocock has also purchased several more of the same breed from the West, and now has a herd of fifteen or twenty of these fine cattle, which present a beautiful sight as they roam over the green meadows of Castalia like a troop of uniformed cavalry, all bearing the same striking marks of white head and red body.

Thus Mr. Boocock is doing a grand service for the stockmen of the South; and this public-spirited gentleman should be sustained in his noble work, which we are glad to learn is meeting with marked success, and will eventually become a leading enterprise in the State.

The visitor to Castalia will now find it like a bit of old England dropped into the lap of Virginia, having all the appointments of a large first-class stock farm, which will give delight to every lover of fine cattle; but more especially it is gratifying to see this old homestead so beautifully perpetuated, retaining its old log cabin and famous spring, which, with its many associations of the past, will always make it dear to the dwellers along the South-West Mountains.

MUSIC HALL

HOME OF THE LATE CAPTAIN JAMES TERRELL

THIS old home, so well remembered as the place where music, joy, and mirth were wont to dwell, as its name indicates, lies contiguous to Castalia, and once formed a part of the Clover Fields estate.

Some ten years after the death of her husband, Colonel Nicholas Meriwether, Margaret Douglas, his widow, married, February 20, 1783, Chiles Terrell.

"Parson" Douglas, of Louisa, her father, sometimes wrote the name "Tyrrell," "Tyrel," or "Terrell," all of which were of Scotch origin. After their marriage they moved and settled upon this portion of the Meriwether grant, which was retained by the widow of Nicholas Meriwether, and consisted of about twelve hundred acres, beginning at the top of the mountain and reaching to the Machunk Creek, the road which passes over Broadhead's Gap to Stony Point being the division-line with the Belvoir estate.

Chiles Terrell must have erected the first house at Music Hall, which was quite a plain framed building. Mrs. Margaret Terrell brought many of the trophies and relics of her husband with her to Music Hall, and for some time the old musket that "Colonel Nick" Meriwether used in the Braddock war was seen there hanging on the wall. By their marriage was one son, James Hunter Terrell, who was born there September 8, 1784, and after the death of his parents succeeded to the Music Hall estate. His mother, Margaret Douglas Terrell, died at Clover Fields, the residence then of her eldest son, Captain William Douglas Meriwether, September 25, 1812. Her son, James Hunter Terrell, married a Northern lady, Mrs. Susan Townley *née* Vibert, of Lynn, Massachusetts. They had no children, but made their home very happy for others, always having several nephews and nieces staying with them, who were very musical. "Uncle Jimmy," as he was universally called, was also passionately fond of music, and was quite a musician himself, playing upon several instruments, hence he named his home Music Hall, as it always resounded to sweet strains and the joyful mirth of youth. Captain Terrell was an officer in the war of 1812, and was also quite prominent in the county. He is mentioned by Bishop Meade as one of a committee to build the new Grace Church.

About 1845, Captain Terrell and his wife made a trip to Massachusetts to see her relations. A lady friend who accompanied them wrote a most amusing and interesting account of the trip, describing the wonder and astonishment of these good, simple-hearted old people at the many sights they saw in the more advanced part of the Union. "Uncle Jimmy," however, was quite restless, and expressed himself as being very glad to get back safely to his old home after his venture upon such a long trip by steam, being the first time he ever rode on the cars.

Such was his kind-heartedness and deep sense of feeling upon the slavery question, that by his will Captain Terrell liberated all of his slaves, eighty-three in number, and devoted his entire Duckinghole estate in Louisa, inherited from his grandfather, Rev. William Douglas, to settling them in Liberia, and in the spring of 1847 these negroes were sent there under the auspices of the "American Colonization Society." This number included a few who were bought or given, that they might not be separated from their husbands or wives. They had a splendid outfit, a free passage, and about three hundred dollars each in money. The writer remembers the departure of these negroes, many of whom were presented with *woollen* gloves and *thick*, heavy clothing, *blankets*, etc., for their tropical home.

Besides owning the Music Hall estate, Captain Terrell had two hundred or more acres of woodland beyond the Machunk, called Clarke's tract, besides inheriting the old homestead in Louisa, Duckinghole, which was the residence of his grandfather, Rev. William Douglas, of Colonial fame. This celebrated farm was not far from Louisa Court-House, and was considered one of the richest sections of the county. It contained about seven hundred and ninety-six acres, which were bought by Mr. Douglas of John Symms in 1770. Mr.

HISTORIC HOMES OF THE

Douglas owned also large bodies of land, more than eleven hundred acres in Goochland County, which was a part of the Cocke estate, bought under the Crown from Governor Spotswood in 1714. This land Mr. Douglas gave to his other grandson, Thomas Meriwether, who lived with him, as by deed dated 1777. As an item of interest, this Cocke tract of two thousand four hundred and ninety-seven acres, lying mostly on James River, was purchased for twelve pounds ten shillings (about sixty-five dollars). The Rev. William Douglas, the grandfather of Captain Terrell, was a most learned divine of the Established Church of England, where he was ordained in 1751. He was a Scotchman, and was educated for the ministry at Edinburgh. He and his family were loyal to the Crown, and did not readily swear allegiance to the colonies; but it was either this or lose by confiscation his large property. Afterwards he became very zealous in establishing the church upon the order of State government. He had an extensive and valuable library brought from Scotland in 1751, and perhaps one of the best in the country at that time. Many of his books have been eagerly sought for and are widely scattered over the country. Mr. Douglas was a teacher of note. Among his pupils were Jefferson, Madison, Wirt, Monroe, and other noted Southern statesmen. He married, in 1735, Miss Nicholas Hunter, niece of Dr. John Hunter, of Edinburgh, so celebrated a hundred years ago.

This Dr. Hunter had also a son, Dr. John

SOUTH-WEST MOUNTAINS

Hunter, who came to Virginia about 1759, settled in Louisa County, and had a large practice in the surrounding counties. Among the long list of his patients, as left by his executor, Rev. William Douglas, we find the name of Sir William Berkeley, governor of the colony, for a medical bill of twelve pounds. Dr. Hunter died in 1762, leaving many descendants. Thus we see how the name of Hunter enters so largely into the Meriwether, Lewis, and Terrell families.

At the death of Captain Terrell, in 1856, the Music Hall mansion and six hundred acres of land were left to his great-nephew and namesake, Dr. James Hunter Minor, whom he had adopted. The lower part of the Music Hall tract and the land beyond the creek, making about eight hundred acres, were left to his wife's niece, Sarah Stranford, who married Howell Lewis, the grandson of Colonel Charles Lewis, who was the son of Colonel Robert Lewis, of Belvoir, who gave this son thirteen hundred and thirty-four acres of land in North Garden, Albemarle. Mr. Howell Lewis's father was the eldest son of this Colonel Charles, and was named Howell; he lived and died at North Garden. Mr. Howell Lewis and his wife, Sarah S. Lewis, lived to a good old age on the Creek farm, where they died.

Dr. Minor greatly added to and improved the Music Hall mansion; indeed, pulling most of it down and building it entirely anew, the rear part being all that is left of the original. It continued to be a most charming place to visit, the sons and daughters of Dr. Minor, with those of Howell Lewis, of the "Creek," inheriting much of the musical talent of their uncle, filling its new halls with sweet strains and pleasant scenes as of old.

Dr. Minor died in 1862, after which Music Hall was bought by its present owner, Mr. Griffith, an English gentleman, who has made further improvements to the building and planted a large portion of the farm in fruit.

The venerable Captain Terrell and his wife lie in the little garden of their old home, and, as the talented author of the "Meriwether Genealogy" says, "The Beatitude used as an epitaph on a joint monument, erected to their memory in the garden at Music Hall by one of the nephews who found in them a father and mother, was never more fitly used than in this instance, ' Blessed are the merciful, for they shall obtain mercy.'" Dr. James Hunter Minor was the son of Samuel Overton Minor, who died in Missouri. He was highly educated as a physician, but did not practise his profession after coming to Music Hall, devoting most of his time to agriculture. In 1843 he married Miss Mary W. Morris, of the Green Springs, Virginia. Of their marriage were:

1. James Hunter Minor; married Ida Lake.
2. Elizabeth Minor; married Robert W. Lewis, of Castalia, now of Richmond, Virginia.
3. William Overton Minor; married Miss Clarke, of California. He was circuit judge in California.
4. Thomas S. Minor; merchant of Charlottesville, Virginia.
5. Rachel C. Minor.
6. Anne Laurie Minor; died young.

BELVOIR

THE HOME OF THE NELSONS

IN our several sketches of the noted homesteads of this Piedmont region, famous as having been the country-seats of noble men and women of the past, we cannot omit to speak more minutely of Belvoir, of which mention has frequently been made in these pages, though its famous old mansion, which sheltered so many of Virginia's statesmen, has long since disappeared, its site being scarcely identified. A complete history of the place would take us back to a very early period, almost to the first settlement of the county, as we find it mentioned about the year 1700, at which time Colonel Robert Lewis moved from New Kent County after his marriage with Jane Meriwether and located on this part of the Meriwether tract.

The exact location of the first Belvoir house, as built by Colonel Robert Lewis, is not known; the " Page Genealogy" states, " The remains of the old Lewis family burying-ground were for a long time to be seen, but nearer the mountain than the house built by Colonel John Walker." Doubtless it was upon one of the higher slopes of the mountain, hence its name " Belle Voir" (beautiful to see). Colonel Lewis came into a large portion of the Nicholas Meriwether estate by marriage with his eldest daughter. He was a prominent officer in the Revolution, and was also in the House of Burgesses. After the death of Colonel Lewis, in 1744, he left his home-place, Belvoir, to his second son, Colonel Nicholas Lewis, who had married the eldest daughter of Dr. Thomas Walker, of Castle Hill. But we find that some time during the Revolution this Nicholas Lewis exchanged lands with John Walker, the eldest son of Dr. Tom Walker, and moved to The Farm, near Charlottesville, where he died. Colonel John Walker, however, did not live in the old Lewis house under the mountain, which was probably a very rude log affair, but built his first house on the level plain near the present residence of Mr. Longfield, and not far from old Walker's Church, which was so called by his name, he having given the land upon which it stood, and which was surveyed by Peter Jefferson, the father of President Thomas Jefferson. The first house that Colonel Walker built was a framed one of the old-fashioned type. We give the following interesting account of it as taken from the "Page" book: "Hon. Colonel John Walker married Elizabeth Moore in 1764, and it was about that time that he built his first house. This house was taken down when the second house was built and moved to Milton, on the Rivanna River, Albemarle County, Virginia. It was afterwards moved to its present location near Cobham, same county, and is the same that was occupied by Howell Lewis. The second house

SOUTH-WEST MOUNTAINS

was built in 1790. This was destroyed by fire in the autumn of 1836. It was thought that the fire was occasioned by a defective flue (loose mortar in the chimney) in the garret, as it was first discovered at that point adjoining the south-west chimney. There were four rooms on the first floor and three rooms up-stairs on the second floor. Above this was a very large garret. About fifty yards north-east from the house was the kitchen, and at the same distance south-west was an outhouse or office. Still farther south-west were stables near the mountain road. Just in rear of the house was an ornamental garden, and behind this was the kitchen-garden, At the north corner was a lot planted in fine trees and shrubs, and at the northern extremity of the latter was the cemetery. The road, with magnificent oaks and poplars on each side, wound gracefully along from the house to the public highway that runs between Gordonsville and Charlottesville, and entered it a little east of a point opposite old Walker's (now Grace) Church." The first house of Colonel Walker, which it speaks of as having been moved to Milton, where Hon. Francis Walker once lived, is still standing on the old Creek farm near the Machunk Creek, where the late Howell Lewis lived. As an interesting incident connected with it there was, and may possibly be still seen, on some of the panes of glass in the windows, cut with a diamond, the names of "Elizabeth Moore" and "Ann Kinlock"; the former being the name of Colonel Walker's wife and the latter the name of his only daughter. It is remarkable that through all the movings of the old building these panes should have remained unbroken over ninety years.

The beautiful grove and avenue of forest-trees spoken of, stretching from the Belvoir house to the church, were in after-years cut down and the entire field put in tobacco by Dr. Tom Meriwether, who had inherited three hundred and fifty acres of the Belvoir tract through his wife. The Hon. William C. Rives, while riding by and seeing the destruction, said jocularly, "Dr. Tom ought to have left one tree on which to hang himself for such a ruthless act."

Colonel John Walker was a very prominent man during the Revolution. He was the confidential aide to General Washington, and afterwards Senator in the United States Congress from Virginia in 1790. Such was his great activity in all revolutionary measures that he was an especial object of capture by Tarleton in his memorable raid, one half of his forces going to Belvoir and the other seeking Castle Hill on their way to Monticello, but the illustrious game was not found at Belvoir. In a private letter of General Washington to Governor Patrick Henry in 1777 he speaks in very high terms of Colonel Walker, whom he had intrusted with important military affairs.

Colonel Walker married Elizabeth Moore, daughter of Bernard Moore, of King William County, Virginia. She was a granddaughter of

SOUTH-WEST MOUNTAINS

Colonel Alexander Spotswood, governor of the colony and founder of the famous Moore House at Yorktown, Virginia.

Colonel Walker and his wife both died in December of 1809, he at Orange Court-House, while on his way to Philadelphia to undergo surgical treatment, and she at Belvoir. Belvoir then descended to their only grandchild, Eliza Kinlock, who married, in 1799, Judge Hugh Nelson, fifth son and child of Governor Thomas Nelson, of Yorktown, Virginia.

The second Belvoir house, built by Colonel Walker in 1790, was of more modern pretensions and much larger than the first. A cut of it is given in the "Page" book, showing it to be quite elaborate in style and architecture for that day. Though much of its handsome furniture and large library was destroyed when burnt in 1836, yet the fine old English organ, which was brought over from England by the Walkers, was taken apart and thrown out of the windows. It was afterwards presented to Grace Church by Mrs. William C. Rives, and did good service there for many years.

Judge Hugh Nelson married Eliza Kinlock in 1799, but did not move to Belvoir until after Colonel Walker's death in 1809. This most distinguished of Virginia's sons was first Speaker of the Virginia House of Delegates, then judge of the Federal court, Presidential elector in 1809, Representative in the United States Congress 1811–23, and was afterwards appointed minister to Spain by President Monroe. One of the most interesting relics connected with Judge Nelson was formerly to be seen at Clover Fields, where his son the late F. K. Nelson lived,—it being an autograph letter from President Monroe, giving him minute directions as to his course while at the Court of Madrid, thus putting into practice his celebrated " Monroe Doctrine." This showed even then with what difficulty our amicable relations with Spain were maintained; but the delicate details were most successfully and adroitly carried out by Judge Nelson with a dignity and impression which quite surprised and overcame the intrigues of that subtle nation.

Judge Nelson was a courtly, handsome gentleman in appearance, an eloquent speaker, and entertained most sumptuously the many who visited Belvoir, especially those of the clergy and legal profession. He was greatly admired and esteemed by Mr. Jefferson, who consulted him frequently on the great Missouri question, and wrote him many letters in 1820 concerning the terrible sacrifice of property under forced sales in Virginia at that time.

Judge Nelson was prominent and active in the church, as have been many of his children and grandchildren since. Among the latter is the Right Reverend C. Kinlock Nelson, Bishop of Georgia.

The Hon. Judge Nelson died in 1836, just previous to the burning of his elegant dwelling, which was never afterwards rebuilt by any of the family. Judge and Mrs. Nelson left a family of nine children,—five sons and four daughters,—many of whom or their descendants are still living in Albemarle County.

After his death the Belvoir estate was divided among five of his children. Dr. Robert W. Nelson, of Charlottesville, his fifth son, obtained the home-place; to Francis K. Nelson, the Peachylorum farm, now Rougemont, lying next to Castle Hill; to his fourth son, Keating S. Nelson, the Greenwood farm; his second daughter, Ann Carter Nelson, who married Dr. Tom Meriwether, receiving the Kinloch farm.

In 1846, Dr. Robert W. Nelson sold his portion, including the old homestead, to the late Colonel D. C. Carver, who erected there a small plain building upon nearly the same site where the Belvoir mansion stood. This building, strange to say, was also burnt. This portion of the tract was afterwards bought by Mr. Longfield, who has since built a neat, tasty dwelling not very far from the site of the old Belvoir mansion.

Mr. Longfield married a Miss Hite, daughter of the late Dr. W. M. Hite, who lived and died at the Kinloch farm. He was very closely connected with the old Walker family, so these lands are still in possession of their descendants.

The old Belvoir burying-ground, where so many of the Meriwethers, Walkers, and Nelsons lie, who were such prominent actors during the stirring events of the past, is still well preserved by a substantial brick wall around it, and their graves marked by marble stones. Here the visitor

HISTORIC HOMES

can almost read the entire history and genealogy of this section upon these monuments, which are all that is left to mark the glory of this historic spot; yet the stately tower of Grace Church rises just opposite old Belvoir as a silent witness to the faith of those who sleep in these tombs, marking as it does the site of the Colonial church building in the time of the Walkers, where many generations of these noted families along the mountains have worshipped, and which will perpetuate for generations to come the memory of Belvoir, the once grand old home of him who gave the land upon which it stands. But we miss the avenue of stately elms which led from the church to the house, and the fine old Belvoir mansion as it sat so conspicuously on the broad plane which crowns the hill, filled as it was with relics of the past, which has passed away forever, closing one of the brightest and most noted homes in Albemarle.

KINLOCH

KINLOCH

THE HOME OF DR. TOM MERIWETHER.

ANOTHER lovely home of the Meriwethers was Kinloch. While neither ancient in construction nor venerable in appearance, it is yet a spot with many happy memories clustering around it, memories of charming days when some of the most brilliant men of the period were wont to gather there, and by their ready wit and fine conversational powers delight and fascinate the many relatives, friends, and neighbors who were constantly filling its halls.

We have already noted the family homestead of Clover Fields, and traced the family history of Captain William D. Meriwether, with the disposition of his large landed estate, which embraced the plantations of Cismont, Clover Fields, Castalia, and Music Hall, each of which stretched from the summit of the South-West Mountains far down to the Machunk Creek. We have thus seen that William Hunter and his two daughters, Mary Walker and Margaret Douglas, inherited most of the home estate. We come now to his youngest son, Thomas Warner Meriwether, who was born at Clover Fields in 1803.

To him was given a plantation on the east side of Clover Fields, which is now known as Clover

Hill, upon which his daughter, the present Mrs. M. N. Macon, now resides. This son, Thomas W., after graduating with high honors at the University of Pennsylvania, Philadelphia, as a physician, married, in 1824, Ann Carter Nelson, sister of the late Francis K. Nelson, and also of Keating S. Nelson, of Fredericksburg, and Dr. R. W. Nelson, of Charlottesville, who were sons of the Hon. Hugh Nelson, of Belvoir.

"Dr. Tom," as he was universally called, settled for a time at Clover Fields and there began the practice of his profession, his little office in the yard still standing as he left it; but after the death of his father-in-law and a division of the Belvoir estate he moved there in 1839 and built upon a portion of it the present mansion, which he called Kinloch, in honor of the Kinloch family of South Carolina, from whom his wife was descended, she being the granddaughter of Francis Kinloch, a Scotchman, who settled very early at Charleston. The name Kinloch was always given the Scotch sound of *Kinlaw*.

The connection of Dr. Meriwether with the high and distinguished family of Nelson, whose prominence in the early annals of Virginia history shines forth in such brilliant colors, leads us to turn for a moment in contemplation of the beautiful character of his wife, Ann Carter Nelson. She was the second daughter of the Hon. Hugh Nelson of the United States Congress from 1811 to 1823. She was also the granddaughter of Governor Thomas Nelson, of Yorktown, and was named for her aunt, Ann Carter, of Shirly, on the James River, who was a sister of the celebrated Robert Carter, known as "King Carter" of historic fame, and who was intimately connected with the Lee family. (See Mead's "Lee Family of Virginia.")

Mrs. Ann Meriwether bore many of the striking characteristics of her illustrious ancestors, having a gentleness of spirit and loving disposition with a cultivated, brilliant, and well-stored mind. She was well fitted for the genial companionship of Dr. Meriwether; her loyalty to her Scotch descent always asserted itself, while she carried with not undue pride the distinguished honors of the Nelson family.

"Dr. Tom" entered at once upon a large practice, it being at a time when there was no physician nearer than Charlottesville on the one side and Gordonsville on the other, with the exception of Dr. Everett, Sr., up to 1840, thus extending for a circuit of twenty miles; and his horses' hoofs were heard to clatter over the hills and mountains from Stony Point to Louisa Court-House, and even far into Fluvanna.

After the destruction of the famous Belvoir mansion in 1836 the prestige of social delight seemed to fall upon Kinloch, where wit and humor and the repartee of cultivated minds would resound.

On the site of the Kinloch mansion once stood an overseer's house, built by the first settlers of Belvoir. It stood in a grove of forest oaks upon the slope of a gentle hill, at the foot of which starts a bold spring. The present mansion is of more modern pretensions than of the Colonial period; yet the plain two-story frame building put up by Dr. Meriwether was in marked contrast to the more recent additions made to it, which, with vine-embowered portico and enlarged hall and rooms, make it a very attractive retreat.

As the youthful sons and daughters of "Dr. Tom" grew up the house was always filled with a joyous, pleasant company of kindred and friends. Here mirth reigned supreme, and both old and young were made to feel the true, hearty welcome of its host and hostess.

Besides his large and extensive practice, Dr. Meriwether was a most successful farmer. This portion of the original Walker tract was always esteemed the best, and its fertility was still further enhanced by judicious cultivation upon strictly scientific principles, which was rarely done at that day, as "book-farming" was considered by the average Virginia farmer as impracticable; but being a firm disciple of the *elder* Ruffin, whose writings in the *Farmers' Register* he studied as faithfully as his medical text-books, "Dr. Tom" proved by his large crops of corn, wheat, and tobacco the successful application of science to agriculture, and, like his noted uncle, Thomas Meriwether, of Louisa County, gained a celebrity in the market for his fine " mountain tobacco," which was often shipped to Europe, the bills of lading for which are still preserved.

But the extensive medical practice of "Dr. Tom" never yielded the rich pecuniary reward its magnitude would imply. Much of his practice among the poorer class was gratuitous, his tender, sympathetic heart never permitting him to press a bill. As an instance of this, a poor neighbor said one day to him, " Dr. Tom, I can't pay all of your bill." " How much can you pay?" inquired the doctor. " I can only pay half of it," replied the man. " Oh, well," said the good doctor, " strike off the other half and call it even." Thus it was with nearly all of his many poor patients. His great solicitude for the health of his more delicate neighbors, in always suggesting the right time for thicker shoes and flannels, or giving a hint about sitting in draughts or exposing to dampness, was in marked contrast to the spirit of the present profession, who are always watchful of the *main chance.*

This solicitude for the health of every one by " Dr. Tom" was once experienced by the writer when, as a small boy, meeting the doctor on the road, he was made to sit on a stump while the doctor dismounted and began to scrub and scrape a very dirty set of teeth, at the same time giving a lecture on cleaning teeth. After getting through he said, " There, sir, now keep them so!"

At another time, during the prevalence of typhoid fever among the negroes, he carried in his pocket one of the elegant family silver spoons with which to administer the medicine. On a remonstrance by some of the family, who suggested a pewter spoon, "Dr. Tom" replied, "No; it must be the same as we would use."

These little peculiarities marked his justness, combined with a charitable disposition such as was exemplified upon every occasion.

Dr. Meriwether was originally a Democrat, but when the Whig party started in 1840, he became an intense admirer of Henry Clay, and ever afterwards affiliated with that party. It was during the exciting campaign of 1844-45, between Clay and Polk, when Dr. Meriwether became so enthusiastic and sure of Mr. Clay's election that he caused to be erected a large "Clay" flag at his gate. During the night, however, some of his Democratic neighbors cut it down, where it was found the next morning trailing in the dust. Not to be outdone, "Dr. Tom," with a few other good Whigs, secured an extra long and stout pole, which Mr. Keating S. Nelson, who was an active young man, nailed to the top of a very tall oak-tree at the doctor's gate on the public road, and, having secured it by bands of iron, he then sawed off all the lower limbs and *tarred* the tree! There the flag waved triumphantly for several years, and though Mr. Clay was not elected, yet "Dr. Tom" would rejoice over his Democratic neighbors that his flag was still flying. The flag was completely worn out, but the pole was seen there ten years afterwards, and possibly some of it is there to this day. But "Dr. Tom" was not so excessive in his politics as was his cousin Peter, with whom he would be sure to have a heated argument whenever they met. His enthusiasm was always more strikingly exhibited when upon literary or scientific subjects. Having a classic mind, which was imbued with a love for the poetical and beautiful, like the celebrated Dr. Samuel Johnson, of England, he was fond of surrounding himself with similar congenial spirits, like the Hon. William C. Rives, Dr. Mann Page, General William F. Gordon, Colonel Thomas J. Randolph, Frank Nelson, and many others, who would frequently grace his hospitable board. On these occasions none could hear the ready bon-mots and hearty laugh of "Dr. Tom" without feeling the keen zest of humor which would be imparted.

Dr. Meriwether early became a member of the Presbyterian church, though his father as well as most of the family were Episcopalians; yet his father, "Captain Billy" Meriwether, did not unite with the church of his forefathers until late in life; he and his young kinswoman, Jane Walker Page, kneeling together, were confirmed by the venerable Bishop Meade in old Walker's Church. It formed a touching picture, the patriarch of seventy-five and the lovely girl of fifteen, both of whom passed away soon afterwards.

The strong convictions of the Presbyterian faith were doubtless received by Dr. Meriwether through his intimacy with the celebrated Dr. Skinner, of Philadelphia, while under his instruction as a medical student; but though strong in the faith, yet the casual observer would never suppose he was other than an ardent Episcopalian from his constant attendance upon the services of Walker's Church and his hearty co-operation in every movement for its growth and improvement, and, more than all, his great love and admiration for its pastor, the Rev. E. Boyden.

It was an amusing sight to see such grave men as " Dr. Tom" Meriwether, F. K. Nelson, J. W. Campbell, Howell Lewis, and many others of the staid farmers of the neighborhood, swinging like a parcel of school-boys upon long levers and shouting lustily to the teams and men, in a vain attempt by the neighbors to move old Walker's Church building to the rear after the completion of the new building; but the old frame could not be moved; it was on too firm a foundation; so " Dr. Tom" and the committee agreed to pull it to pieces and rebuild it in the rear of the new church for the benefit of the colored people; but the colored brothers rebelled. " Dey didn't want no white church in front o' dem; dey wa'n't gwine take no back seat in hebben, no how;" so the old frame was sold to some farmer for a more irreligious purpose.

Dr. Meriwether died in 1862 at Clover Fields, his birthplace, from an attack of pneumonia, contracted while nursing a patient there. His funeral sermon was preached at South Plains Presbyterian Church by the Rev. Mr. Beach, and also at Walker's Church by the Rev. E. Boyden, both taking the same text,—" Mark the perfect man, and behold the upright; for the end of that man is peace." It is needless to say that large crowds

SOUTH-WEST MOUNTAINS

attended on both occasions to attest their love for this "beloved physician," who was laid with his forefathers in the Clover Fields graveyard.

The seven children of Dr. Thomas Meriwether and Anne Carter Nelson are:

1. Dr. William Douglas Meriwether; died in Tennessee, 1880; married, first, Phœbe Gardner, of Richmond, Virginia, 1847, from whom were Mary Gardner; married Mr. Wallace, of Kentucky. Thomas Warner, of Norwalk, Connecticut; married, September 1, 1886, Alice Emma Blandford. Isabella, lives with her sister, Mrs. Wallace, at University of Virginia. Dr. Douglas Meriwether married, second, Anne W. (called Nannie) Page (see "Page" book); she died at Culpeper, Virginia, 1873, leaving one child, Evelyn.
2. Mildred Nelson Meriwether; married, in 1856, George W. Macon, of Tufton, Albemarle; died 1880. Their children are: 1. Thomas W. Macon; Charlotte N. Macon; married Frank M. Randolph, of Clover Fields, January 17, 1883; 2. Littleton Macon; 3. George W. Macon, of Clover Hill farm; 4. Douglas Macon, M.D., now of New Jersey.
3. Anne Kinloch Meriwether; married, December 24, 1850, Frederick W. Page, of Millwood, Albemarle, Virginia.
4. Elizabeth Meriwether; married, 1853, N. H. Massie, of Charlottesville, Virginia; no issue.
5. Charlotte Nelson Meriwether; married, 1865, Thomas Jefferson Randolph, Jr., and was his second wife; died 1876, leaving one daughter, Mary Walker Randolph, who married her cousin, Dr. William Randolph, of Charlottesville, Virginia.
6. Thomas W. Meriwether, Jr.; died single, 1862.
7. Jane Meriwether; died in infancy.

Of the above children of Dr. Meriwether there is but one now living, Mrs. Mildred Nelson

Macon, the widow of the late George W. Macon, who still resides at Clover Hill with her son, George W. Macon, Jr., who has made the old homestead to "blossom as the rose." Clover Hill was a part of the Clover Fields tract, given "Dr. Tom" by his father, Captain William D. Meriwether, and is one of the few spots of the old Meriwether grant retained by the descendants.

Mrs. Macon is said to strongly resemble in features and manner her great-grandmother, Mary Walker, who married Nicholas Lewis, of The Farm, near Charlottesville, and by her eagerness to fight the British and her sway of the home circle won the sobriquet of "Captain Moll." Mrs. Macon shows by her firm, impressive manner, her vivacious conversation, her literary tastes, and her gentle and loving consideration for others many of the beautiful traits of both the Meriwethers and Walkers.

The many grandchildren of Dr. Tom Meriwether are scattered over our country, filling honorable stations in life; yet it is a sad fact that not a foot of the once vast Meriwether patent of seventeen thousand acres is now held under the name of *Meriwether*.

The entire Kinloch farm has passed from the family, and yet it is fortunately owned by a descendant of another historic family, the Everetts, of Belmont. Thus the name of Everett is again linked with the Walker lands as it was nearly a century ago, when the elder Dr. Everett was guardian of Judith Page Walker, who afterwards

SOUTH-WEST MOUNTAINS

was Mrs. William C. Rives, and inherited Castle Hill.

Kinloch was owned, however, just previous to its purchase by its present owner, Mr. Aylett Everett, by Dr. Walker Maury Hite, who was the son of Major Isaac Hite of Revolutionary fame, and was a native of Frederick County, Virginia. Dr. Hite married, in 1836, Mary Eleanor, daughter of Isaac Williams, of Fredericksburg, Virginia, who was a niece of the late Philip Slaughter, D.D., the historiographer. Dr. and Mrs. Hite both died the same day, April 17, 1890, at Kinloch, and were buried in the Grace Church cemetery, in sight of their home.

Their daughter Mary married Mr. Longfield, an English gentleman, who had been a resident of the county for some time. After the death of Dr. Hite they bought and settled upon a part of the Belvoir tract, just opposite to Kinloch, and there built their tasty little home, near the spot where the old Belvoir mansion stood. Dr. Hite was nearly related to the Maurys and Walkers; and it is thus remarkable that the descendants of both these old families should now occupy the lands of the Walkers, and in view of the spot where the Rev. James Maury, first pastor of Walker's Church, preached and was laid.

Kinloch is now owned by Mr. Aylett Everett, a rising and popular young farmer, who is causing its fields and surroundings to assume their former productive appearance. Mr. Everett married Miss Sadie Fry, daughter of the late Captain John Fry,

HISTORIC HOMES

formerly of Richmond, Virginia, from which union they have several children.

Peaceful Kinloch sets as of old, surrounded by draperies of living green, and its lofty trees shed a luxuriance of shade over its sloping lawn; but its noble old oaks, which have always been its pride and so long have sheltered the mansion, are fast showing the lapse of time and are gradually passing away, while the mountain breezes still sigh a requiem through their decayed limbs in remembrance of the happy, peaceful, and prosperous days which have passed over this true type of an old Virginia home.

MERRIE MILL

THE COUNTRY-SEAT OF JOHN ARMSTRONG CHANLER, ESQ.

THOUGH not boasting of any antiquated ancestral mansion with legends of Colonial fame, yet Merrie Mill stands upon historic ground and takes its name from one of the most interesting and ancient landmarks that links the past with the present. This is the old Walker Mill which sits at the foot of the hill upon which the mansion rests and carries on its useful, musical work by the aid of a little stream which flows through the farm. In the time of Colonel John Walker, of Belvoir, who owned all of the land embraced in the present Rougemont, Kinloch, and Belvoir tracts, there was erected here a grist-mill, partly of stone and partly framed, which is said to have been built by a celebrated mechanic named Johnson from Louisa County, who had done much work for " Parson" Douglas of Colonial fame upon his Duckinghole farm. This unique old mill still stands to attest the substantial structures of our forefathers. The first story is of stone, with walls a foot thick; upon this is built another story of wood, its huge timbers being mortised together and fastened with wooden pins. The rough board siding is covered with whip-sawed clapboards put on with hand-wrought nails, and its heart-pine shingles are secured in the same manner.

The durability of the work of early carpenters is thus shown, as the timbers of the old mill are nearly as sound as when first put in, and so firmly put together as to resist the storms of many decades. The story is told that when it was completed the event was celebrated by a grand old Virginia party upon its newly-laid floor, to which the young people far and near attended and thus christened it "Merrie Mill," and right merrily has its old wheel turned ever since to the music of its splashing waters, defying the wear and tear of time or the destruction of war.

It is said that it ground corn for the Colonial army, and is one of the few mills which escaped burning by the British under Tarleton or by the "Yankees" under Sheridan during the civil war. It has supplied the community with bread for more than a century, and still does duty when sufficient water is supplied to its now silent wheel. We are glad to note that Mr. Chanler is about to repair the old mill and again make it useful.

In honor of this ancient old mill and the historic ground upon which it stands Mr. Chanler has named his beautiful country-seat. The history of Belvoir, of which the old mill was once a part, is coeval with that of Castle Hill, which is but a few miles distant, though it is highly probable that the first Belvoir mansion erected by Colonel Robert

THE OLD COLONIAL MERRIE MILL.
On the Merrie Mill Farm

Lewis, which was nearer the mountains, antedates the building of Castle Hill.

All of the land was a part of the celebrated Meriwether grant from George II., but the intricacies through which the property has descended and been divided are many,—Meriwether, Lewis, Walker, Rives, Nelson, Terrell, Minor, and Lewis again, each in their order, until nearly all of the five thousand acres has passed out of the family. Merrie Mill farm was once a part of the Creek farm, both of which formed a part of the Music Hall estate, which was owned by the late Captain James Terrell. At his death the whole Music Hall tract was divided between his nephew, Dr. J. H. Minor, and his wife's niece, Sarah Stanford, who married Howell Lewis, they getting the lower portion, which extended to the Machunk Creek, where they built their home, Creek farm.

In 1857, Mr. Edward S. Pegram, a retired Baltimore merchant, purchased of Mr. John Fry, who had married the eldest daughter of Mr. Howell Lewis, six hundred acres of the Creek farm, most of which was in original timber. Here he erected the present substantial building, which was constructed under his personal supervision, and formed one of the most complete modern structures of the day.

The house is of two stories, forming a T in shape, with artistic entablature of fretted cornice and fluted columns; its interior is spacious, each of its rooms and wide halls above and below are finished in polished chestnut and oak, while every detail is in keeping with its tasty design, and forms one of the most striking and ornamental residences along the mountains.

This place was first named Edgefield, where Mr. Pegram lived for many years, dispensing the hospitalities and charities of a truly refined and Christian home.

About 1880 Edgefield was sold to Dr. Bird, a retired English officer, who had been deputy surgeon-general in the East Indian service. This gentleman greatly improved the farm, setting out large orchards and vineyards, and embellished the lawn with many evergreens and ornamental trees, which have since attained a magnificent growth and give to the place quite an English ancestral aspect.

After the death of Dr. Bird, in 1890, the farm was purchased by its present owner, Mr. John Armstrong Chanler, of the New York law firm of Maxwell Chanler & Co. This gentleman has still further added many acres to the original tract, making the present Merrie Mill farm to consist of about one thousand acres, stretching over a wide area of hill and dale and extended woodland, which forms a grand park of original growth, through which the approach to the house is gained.

Seated at an elevation of four hundred and fifty feet above the sea-level, Merrie Mill forms one of the few homesteads which face the mountains, and from which is gained a grand view of its entire South-West range; and though the houses situated along the higher mountain slopes may boast of a more extended view of the lower lands, yet nothing

THE BATHING-POOL AT MERRIE MILL.

SOUTH-WEST MOUNTAINS

surpasses the solemn grandeur of the "everlasting hills" as seen from the Merrie Mill door-steps. The mansion itself stands upon an elevated plain, on each side of which is a valley, and through these valleys wind the streams that turn the ancient mill in the distance.

On each side of the farm rises majestic oaks of the original forest, along the eastern side of which is still to be seen traces of an old road, which was once known as the "Marquis road," along which tradition says La Fayette travelled when on his visit to Charlottesville, and the same road was traversed by a portion of Tarleton's troops when on his raid to Monticello. One of the most attractive and interesting features of Merrie Mill, and so uncommon to most country places, is its bathing-pool, a cut of which is given. At a great expense Mr. Chanler has turned the waters of a bold, clear spring at the foot of the hill into a pool of fifty feet in length, twenty in width, and from four to six feet in depth. The bottom and sides are lined with tin, while at one end stand tasty dressing-rooms for ladies and gentlemen, and at the other an elevated platform and spring-board from which the athletic swimmer can make a graceful dive. The whole is surrounded by a balustrade, with every appliance to aid the young swimmer or rescue from drowning the unwary youth in their first efforts.

This delightful pool of limpid water is gratuitously thrown open to the young people twice a week; and it is needless to say nothing can exceed the pleasure which this boundless gift bestows upon his neighborhood.

Mr. Chanler has also proved a liberal patron to the handsome Gothic Grace Church which stands in view of his country-seat and adjoins his grounds; it was his thoughtful, generous spirit that enabled its congregation to rebuild more beautifully than before their loved church edifice after its destruction by fire in 1894, he having placed an insurance upon it of twelve thousand dollars.

Mr. Chanler has unostentatiously been a generous contributor to every enterprise for the welfare of the community, and has aided in a quiet way many of his less fortunate neighbors; it is therefore no surprise that he is held in great love and admiration by his fellow-citizens wherever he is known. Mr. Chanler's liberality, however, has not been confined to Virginia alone. Being himself a great lover of art, he has endowed most handsomely an institution in New York for the encouragement of poor artists and those struggling in literary pursuits. Thus his great wealth has been made to benefit his fellow-men, and who shall say he has not fulfilled the divine law?

Having sojourned in Paris, Berlin, and other parts of Europe, Mr. Chanler has adorned his beautiful home with many choice pieces of statuary, paintings, and rare books from the old country. The lover of the antique can also see here many interesting relics of the past, among which are some of Thomas Jefferson's furniture, besides old books, papers, and curios from different parts of the world.

SOUTH-WEST MOUNTAINS

Merrie Mill in summer-time is an idealistic spot, its beautiful lawn bedecked with stately evergreens and fruit-trees, which almost conceal the mansion in their wealth of foliage, its sensuous perfume of fragrant flowers, the song of birds, the luxuriantly oriental *chaise-à-bras*, which tempts the visitor to delightful *abandon*, while on every side rich paintings and books pander to the love of literature and art. Certainly there is no place under the shadow of the South-West Mountains which so readily fills the dream of the poet,—

> "A wilderness of sweets; for Nature here
> Wanton'd as in her prime, and played at will
> Her virgin fancies, pouring forth more sweet,
> Wild above rule or art, enormous bliss."

The family of Mr. Chanler is one of the oldest and most distinguished of New York State. He was born in New York, October 10, 1862, the son of John Winthrop Chanler and Margaret Astor Ward, grandson of Samuel Ward and Emily Astor, and great-grandson of William B. Astor and Margaret Armstrong, and also great-grandson of John Armstrong and Miss Livingston.

John Armstrong was a native of Pennsylvania, and was a colonel during the French and Indian wars. On March 1, 1776, he was commissioned brigadier-general in the Pennsylvania Line, and was engaged in the battles of Brandywine, Germantown, and other actions during the Revolution. He resigned April 4, 1777, and became a member of the first Congress. He died at Carlisle,

HISTORIC HOMES

Pennsylvania, March 9, 1795. Mr. Chanler is a member of the "Sons of the Revolution," and also the "Society of Fine Arts" and other literary institutions in New York City. He graduated when quite young in law, and is a prominent member of the New York bar.

Besides his legal practice, Mr. Chanler has large interests in cotton and iron factories in North Carolina and other Southern States, and his investments are scattered through many parts of the Union.

Mr. Chanler has never entered politics or aspired to office, though frequently urged to do so by his many friends. His tastes lie more in the quiet pleasures of literary and artistic pursuits, untrammelled by the ties of office; yet his political feelings have always been with the South, and of a broad, conservative character.

Unostentatious in manner, of a bounteous hospitality, a genial, happy disposition, such is a slight sketch of the owner of the beautiful Merrie Mill farm, who for one so young has attained an enviable position in the public eye, and is one of the prominent men of our time.

ROUGEMONT

THE HOME OF THE DICKINSONS

SEATED at an elevation of seven hundred and six feet on one of the highest slopes of the South-West range is Rougemont. It enjoys an altitude higher than any of the old homesteads between Charlottesville and Gordonsville, and commands a far-reaching view of the eastern horizon, while rising abruptly from its rear towers Rougemont Mountain, thirteen hundred and seventy-six feet above the sea-level. This place was once called Peachylorum, doubtless in honor of the Peachy family, with whom the Walkers intermarried at an early date. Lying as it does contiguous to Castle Hill, it once formed a part of the Belvoir estate, which was cut off about the year 1764 by Dr. Thomas Walker and given to his eldest son, Hon. John Walker. The Hon. Hugh Nelson next succeeded to the estate, and gave the Peachylorum tract to his eldest son, Francis K. Nelson, who doubtless built there the first residence, about the year 1824. He lived at Peachylorum until his second marriage, in 1843, his second wife being Margaret Douglas Meriwether, of Clover Fields, to which place he removed, and there died. In 1845 Peachylorum was bought by Charles J. Meriwether, the brother of his second wife, who married a Miss Miller. They lived at Peachylorum for many years, beautifying the place and making it a lovely resort for their many relatives and friends.

Mr. Meriwether outlived all of his brothers and sisters, and is still remembered as a true type of the Meriwether family,—firm and decided in every opinion, with a most congenial and hospitable disposition. He was a delegate to the Episcopal Convention of Virginia every year from its commencement in 1830 to his death. They had no children, but lived for the happiness of others. They travelled extensively, visiting Europe and the Holy Land, as well as over the greater portion of the United States, and imparted the great knowledge gained by their careful observations to the advancement of the youth around them. After their death Peachylorum was sold in 1854 to Captain George C. Dickinson, of New York.

When Captain Dickinson took possession, the name of the place was changed to Rougemont by suggestion of Mrs. William C. Rives, of Castle Hill, as being more appropriate, significant of the soil on which it stands.

Captain Dickinson made vast improvements to the old building, which was quite small, and under his skill and taste as an architect was greatly enlarged and modernized, having spacious halls and rooms, with the addition of a large dancing-saloon, which was often the scene of most sumptuous entertainments, such as won for it among

SOUTH-WEST MOUNTAINS

the *beau monde* of that day a wide-spread celebrity for enchanting festivity.

The mansion now stands most conspicuously amid rich forest-trees, forming a beautiful picture as seated on its lofty eminence surrounded by sloping hills, with the mountain for its background. In 1846 it was discovered that this high hill upon which it sits was formed of solid granite, lying but a few feet from its surface, and when the present Grace Church was planned by Mrs. William C. Rives, the building was constructed entirely of this granite, many tons of which were quarried not far from the Rougemont mansion. This granite has since proved its superior quality by resisting the wear and tear of time or destruction by fire. Rougemont Mountain is also famous as being the spot where the last *wolf* of the South-West Mountains was killed, the skin of which was stuffed and kept for many years at Clover Fields. The writer can well remember this exciting event, which caused the youth of that day to display their bravery in the hunt, and the rejoicings of the farmers over its capture, it having caused much loss to their flocks.

George Codwise Dickinson was born in the city of New York in 1832. He was a direct descendant of the old Knickerbocker family, the first settlers of Manhattan Island. He was also in direct line connected with the Van Rensselaers, Byvanckes, Codwises, Van Ransts, Bleekers, and other celebrated and ancient families of the State.

Captain Dickinson graduated quite early as a civil engineer, and rose rapidly in his profession, attaining a high position on many public works. He was a prominent member of the "American Society of Civil Engineers," who, after his death, published a handsome tribute to his memory. At the commencement of the civil war in 1861, he was commissioned in the engineer service of the State of Virginia, and assigned to duty in the forts at Gloucester Point and York River. In 1862 he entered the service of the Confederate States, and for some time was engaged as division engineer in the surveys and construction of the Piedmont Railroad in Virginia and North Carolina. From May, 1863, until the close of the war he was on duty as captain of engineers in the Army of Northern Virginia, serving in Pender's division under General A. P. Hill. In 1890 he had charge, as assistant engineer, of the Hudson Suspension Bridge and New England Railway; also on the Peekskill Suspension Bridge, over the Hudson River. In 1891, and to the time of his death, he was chief engineer of the Broadway and West Virginia Mining Company Railroad. He also held positions on the Baltimore and Ohio, Chesapeake and Ohio, New York Central, and Hudson River Railroads, and was city engineer of Portsmouth, Ohio, besides doing much private work. We quote the high testimonial which his work elicited from the "American Society of Civil Engineers."

"In all the various lines of his profession in which Mr. Dickinson was engaged he took a genuine delight and gave his undivided attention. He was exceedingly methodical and accurate, careful, a close reasoner, and honest in all his work, and his results could always be relied upon. His early habits of study continued through his business life, and he devoted many hours of each day before the active discharge of his duties to preparation for them and to quiet study."

In 1862, Captain Dickinson married Kate Baldwin, the daughter of the late Herman Baldwin, of Richmond, Virginia, who was at one time cashier of the Mechanics' Bank, Wall Street, New York. He moved to Richmond, Virginia, in 1835, where he built up a large and prosperous business. Mrs. Dickinson had a sister, Emmeline, who married George Otis Sweet, of South Carolina. She has recently died at the advanced age of eighty-two years. The late Horace L. Kent, of Richmond, also married one of the sisters of Mrs. Dickinson.

From this union of Captain Dickinson and Kate Baldwin were five sons and one daughter:

1. Rev. Thomas Gilford Dickinson, pastor of the King Avenue Methodist Church, Columbus, Ohio.
2. Helen Augusta Dickinson; only daughter. Died January 17, 1892, a few days prior to the death of her father.
3. Charles Edward Dickinson, Cobham, Virginia; civil engineer.
4. Dr. John Byvanck Dickinson; a prominent physician of Boston, Massachusetts.
5. Richard Dickinson. Died in 1893.
6. George Otis Dickinson. Died January 3, 1897.

HISTORIC HOMES

Captain G. C. Dickinson died January 24, 1892. His grave and that of his sons and only daughter lie in the Grace Church cemetery, which his hands laid off. Their graves are marked by a handsome and massive monument of Vermont granite, around which are constantly kept fresh and fragrant flowers by loving hands. Captain Dickinson had a younger brother, Edward Tompkins Dickinson, who resides in Châtenay, France.

All the members of the family have been noted for their high culture, noble bearing, and great success in their various professions. Captain Dickinson was a liberal and enthusiastic supporter of the Episcopal Church, being for many years senior warden of the beautiful Gothic Grace Church which stands in full view of their attractive home as it sits on the gentle hill Rougemont.

HOPEDALE

THE HOME OF THE BOYDENS

MENTION has been made already in the sketch of Cismont that the Rev. E. Boyden once lived in the old dwelling at the foot of the hill, which he called "The Cottage Rectory," where he lived until the year 1849, when he purchased two hundred and twenty acres of land near the present Grace Church and removed to his new home. This farm belonged to a Miss Lucy Miller, a descendant of a family who had long resided there. They doubtless came from Goochland County, as we find W. Miller was clerk of Goochland Court in 1794, which position has been handed down from father to son to the present day, it being now held by Mr. William Miller and his son Mr. P. G. Miller. This tract of land lies between Castle Hill and Kinloch, and must have formed a part of the Walker tract. A very old but strongly built frame dwelling of one and one-half stories, containing four large rooms, stood not far from the county road; to this Mr. Boyden began to build a brick addition of eight rooms, but which was not entirely completed for some time afterwards. The place, before Mr. Boyden took it, was a galled and barren spot, which was called the "eyesore" of the neighborhood; but it was named Hopedale, as it was bought in *hope*, such as alone sustains the weary toilers of the soil, and but for which the world would cease.

But by skill and shrewdness, combined with a refined and cultivated taste for the beautiful in nature, Mr. Boyden soon made it a most attractive and ornamental home without any great expenditure of money. For many years afterwards Mr. Boyden continued his school which had been formed at the "Cottage Rectory," and under the guidance of his accomplished daughters, aided by skilful teachers, became quite celebrated as a refined home-school for young ladies.

Mr. Boyden was quite an enthusiast in horticulture, planting most of his farm in apple-trees and fruits generally, which yielded quite a large revenue each year.

Hopedale has of late years become an attractive resort for summer visitors to this interesting region. Here they can view the lofty Peter's Mountain on the one hand, near the foot of which nestle Castle Hill and Keswick School, on the other side rise Kinloch, Belvoir, and Bowlesville, with the Gothic tower of Grace Church peeping above the distant tree-tops; while before the door expands a wide table landscape, where hill and dale, interrupted with woodland, form a pleasing view.

The family of Boyden stands pre-eminently conspicuous through the whole history of our country, beginning as early as 1630, when three

SOUTH-WEST MOUNTAINS

brothers of the name came from England and settled upon the spot where the city of Boston, Massachusetts, now stands. In 1660 two of these brothers with their families removed and settled at Worcester, Massachusetts; the third one also moved, to New Jersey, where the name gradually changed to Borden, from which Bordentown was named. In 1730 three families of the name emigrated to Vermont, the heads of which were Daniel, William, and James Boyden, brothers. Daniel and James settled near Guilford, and William at Drummerstown, Vermont. The eldest, Daniel, was grandfather of the subject of this sketch, and was a very devout and good man, who died about 1809. His eldest son, Daniel, was the father of the Rev. E. Boyden, and inherited the well-cultivated farm of his father, who had redeemed it from the wilderness. He died in 1852. The mother of Mr. Boyden was Miss Goodenough, daughter of Ebenezer Goodenough, who lived to be ninety years of age, dying in 1828, a very religious man.

Ebenezer Boyden, of Hopedale, son of Daniel and Tabitha Boyden, of Vermont, was born at Guilford, May 25, 1803. At the age of sixteen he was confirmed by Bishop Griswold. He entered Yale College in 1821, and graduated with honor in 1825. In 1827 he entered the Virginia Theological Seminary at Alexandria, and was ordained deacon at Petersburg by Bishop Moore in 1828. He returned to the seminary and took charge, as editor, for eighteen months, of the

Theological Repository, a monthly magazine, previously edited by the professors. In 1829 he preached for three months in Christ Church, Georgetown, D.C. In January, 1830, he took charge of Trinity Church, Staunton, Virginia, which was a small brick building, a relic of Colonial times, having high square pews, clerk's desk, reading-desk, and pulpit, each rising above the other in the same line, the pulpit being very high above the people.

Staunton was at that time a town of about twelve hundred inhabitants. Prejudice against the Episcopal Church was then quite strong and very general throughout the valley; but by tact, energy, and great effort Mr. Boyden succeeded in establishing it upon a firm footing in the county, and finally in erecting a new church building of larger proportions and more modern appearance in place of the old one. He also gathered funds and built, about six miles distant from Staunton, a neat brick chapel, where he held regular services for two years, and when the bounds of the parish were afterwards established his name was given to it, the building being still known as " Boyden Chapel."

In January, 1832, he married Mary Sheffey, eldest daughter of the Hon. Daniel Sheffey, of Staunton, one of the most noted lawyers of his day and Senator in the United States Congress from Virginia. He was also famous for his benevolent Christian character and large benefactions. Much more could be said of this illustrious statesman did space permit.

SOUTH-WEST MOUNTAINS

On the mother's side, Mrs. Boyden belonged to the Hansons, at one time a wealthy family of Maryland and the District.

Mrs. Boyden was a woman of strong, elevated character and of earnest, devout piety, a model wife and mother. She truly became a helpmate for her husband and fulfilled in the highest degree a clergyman's wife. At a time when missionary zeal was almost extinct her interest in it became intense and expansive, and her personal contributions to the cause were as liberal as the most rigid self-denial could make them. She died honored and beloved in October, 1881.

Near the close of 1832, Mr. Boyden accepted a call to St. Paul's Church, Norfolk, Virginia, where he remained about two years and a half, greatly beloved, building up the congregation and strengthening the church in that place. Owing to failing health caused by the low country, he left Norfolk and took charge of Trinity Church, Cleveland, Ohio. Here he found the work too severe for a delicate constitution, and in November, 1838, he resigned his charge and returned to Virginia.

On June 1, 1839, he became rector of Walker's Church, Albemarle County, having in connection with it St. Ann's Church in the same county. The latter he resigned in 1849, accepting in its stead St. John's Church in Louisa County.

When first taking charge of old Walker's Church, Mr. Boyden found it similar to the one he had previously held in Staunton, Virginia, being of the Colonial style, having high-backed pews and a very lofty pulpit, which admitted of small space between the ceiling and the preacher's head. It was a very rude framed building, many of its clapboards loose and missing, while between the wainscoting many generations of wasps had built their nests, which, upon the approach of spring weather, would send forth swarms of the pestiferous vespidæ, to the great annoyance of pastor and congregation, who would frequently be compelled to beat a retreat.

Here Mr. Boyden labored for many years, working most assiduously for the erection of the beautiful stone building, the corner-stone of which he laid in 1848, and his heart rejoiced to see its completion and consecration in 1855. Mr. Boyden continued to fill the pulpits of his several churches until 1879, when he resigned them, after having served the community faithfully for *forty years!* Nor did the increasing infirmities of old age, which caused this retirement, leave him totally inactive, for he continued in usefulness and good works as long as his strength permitted. In February, 1890, he was attacked with the prevailing epidemic of influenza, from which he could not rally, and on January 15, 1891, he entered into rest, in his eighty-eighth year, at his home, Hopedale, which he had built and beautified. Mr. Boyden was a most forcible preacher, an elegant writer, using the purest diction, and possessed of a clear and wonderful mind; he was of a poetical nature, often clothing his thoughts in verse, a lover of the beautiful in nature, brilliant in imagination, with decidedly original views on the general topics of the day, which would frequently emanate from his pen, and always attract the thinking public.

A handsome memorial window of rich stained glass, in rear of the chancel of the beautifully reconstructed Grace Church, can now be seen, erected to the memory of this beloved pastor by the late Dr. Richard Channing Moore Page, of New York City, which bears the following inscription:

> "REV^D E. BOYDEN.
> Born May 25th, 1803.
> Died January 15th, 1891.
> For forty years the beloved
> Rector of this church."

Just previous to the civil war, when the country was agitated on the slavery question, he wrote a pamphlet, " The Epidemic of the Nineteenth Century," being a strong argument in support of the institution from a scriptural point of view. This coming from a man who had been reared in the hot-bed of abolitionism, but who had seen the falsity of Northern prejudice and the just and humane treatment of the negroes in the South, attracted great attention and comment both North and South, and being irrefutable it had a marked effect. Two of Mr. Boyden's sons entered the ministry of the Episcopal Church. The eldest, Rev. Daniel Hanson Boyden, died in 1871, after having served as chaplain in the Confederate service, which proved fatal to his delicate constitution. The younger son, the Rev. Peter Meriwether Boyden, rector of the church at Boydton,

HISTORIC HOMES

Mecklenburg County, Virginia, for many years, now of Brookville, Maryland. He married, in 1879, Miss Ella W. Smith, daughter of Dr. William Smith, of Goochland, Virginia.

Their five children are:

> 1. Mary Sheffey. 2. Eleanor Shepherd. 3. Adele Pendleton. 4. Rosa Rutherford. 5. Lillian Gordon.

The third son, John Lewis Boyden, farms the old homestead, an honored and respected Christian gentleman. He married, in 1879, Miss Cornelia Payne, of Amherst, daughter of Samuel Spotswood Payne, Esq., a descendant of Governor Spotswood. Mrs. Boyden also claims descent from "Dolly" Madison, the wife of President Madison.

Their children are:

> 1. John Hanson. 2. Bessie Noland. 3. Margaret Douglas.

Four daughters survive their father, the Rev. E. Boyden,—Mary Sheffey, Frances Meriwether, born in the Cismont mansion, Celestine, and Henrietta. The second daughter, Lilla, died February 22, 1890.

It is interesting to note the names of Lewis and Meriwether linked with that of Boyden, who, though of no kindred to the latter, yet now own a part of the soil once trod by General Robert Lewis, of Belvoir, and Colonel Nicholas Meriwether of old; it was in gratitude and admiration for the descendants of these noble families that led Mr. Boyden to name his sons and daughters for those, among whom his children had lived and been reared, as "of the manor born."

CASTLE HILL

THE HOME OF THE RIVESES

IF there is any place by man's creation which approaches the great secret of nature, like the untouched woods or the ocean's roar, which calls forth our solemn admiration—that place is Castle Hill. Let us leave the shimmering fields 'neath an August sun and enter this sylvan retreat, there to bathe in an atmosphere which has created poets and philosophers.

In approaching the domains of Castle Hill from the public highway we course a long avenue formed on each side by lofty cedars and locusts, which extend in graceful curves for nearly a mile. As the mountains are approached we reach an elevated plain, from which a wide expanse of view breaks forth towards the east.

On entering the portals of an extended lawn which stretches for several hundred yards from the house, which even yet can scarcely be seen amidst the dense foliage, one is lifted in a transport of delight while circling through a maze of lofty oaks, drooping ferns, and fragrant evergreens. On every side Nature and Art seem to meet and kiss each other. On the one hand a tangled undergrowth of original forest, while on the other a long stretch of velvet green, dotted here and there with tropical plants, which waft the perfumed air and cooling breeze in joyous welcome towards the visitor, who feels as if approaching some enchanted haven of peaceful rest, such as this beautiful home really possesses.

The stranger who visits Castle Hill for the first time is apt to feel disappointed at not seeing some lofty palatial structure, such as its name implies. The house is scarcely visible at all through the forest of trees until he alights at the foot of its steps, which lead to a wide-spread portico, whose stately Corinthian columns are entwined with English ivy, while on each side towering azalias stand sentinel. Glancing up, one sees a simple, plain two-story brick building, flanked on each side by high windows and glass doors, which lead to extensive conservatories. It is not until entering the wide hall and looking to the rear that one is struck with the beauty of its luxurious space, which the mansion presents in truly castellated style.

The first to catch the eye of the visitor is its many works of art. Wherever one turns—in hall, parlor, or dining-room—he beholds some choice work from the brush of Amélie Rives (now Princess Troubetzkoy) or one of the old masters which adorn its many walls. To one who is familiar with the family history it affords delight to recognize the excellent portraits of the Hon. Mr. and Mrs. William C. Rives, being copies taken by Princess Troubetzkoy from the originals of the celebrated engraver Charles Fendrich in 1838, representing Mr. Rives at the age of forty. Also the fine portraits of his eldest daughter, Mrs. Amélie Louise Sigourney, and her sister, Miss Ella Rives, taken by the famous French artist, Guillaume. One of the most interesting of the family collection is that of the three sons of Mr. Rives,—Francis Robert, William Cabell, and Alfred Landon,—at the ages of ten, seven, and three years. These form a group, presenting a most pleasant, life-like scene, and were taken in Paris in 1832, while Mr. Rives was ambassador from this country.

Many other portraits, landscapes, etchings, and rich *bric-à-brac*, collections of many years of travel in foreign lands, will claim the attention of the visitor, from which he will turn with reluctance.

The second story is gained by a circular stairway, and its rooms are as capacious and lofty as those below. To the left is pointed out the room of Amélie Rives (then Mrs. Chanler), where at the window fronting the lawn stand her little rocking-chair and the table upon which she wrote "The Quick or the Dead?" and many of her other productions. Stepping upon the upper balcony, one here can gain the best view of the wide-spread lawn, stretching forth like a lake of green, with arched elms and evergreens on each side, forming a grand vista, upon which the eye never grows weary of gazing. Descending again to the wide hall below, which extends through the entire building, or rather both buildings, for the front or brick part is comparatively a modern structure, having been built by Mr. Rives in 1824 and more recently improved by his son, Colonel Alfred L. Rives, who has expended large sums in its remodelling and embellishment.

Such is the present Castle Hill mansion as its front presents, and as the visitor will find a

> " Beauty in every stick and stone,
> With nature, too, to call its own."

Passing through its wide hallway to the rear we come to the still more interesting part, its wooden, or the original building of Castle Hill, as erected in the time of Dr. Thomas Walker, 1764. We give quite an accurate view of this old portion, showing its antiquated appearance, with its low roof and small dormer-windows, which have been well preserved, presenting a striking contrast between the architecture of the present and that of more than one hundred years ago. In these diminutive rooms were once assembled such great men as Colonel Peter Jefferson, the father of the President, who also was a frequent visitor, Governor Thomas Nelson, President Madison, and possibly General Washington, for Dr. Walker was intimately associated both publicly and privately with the "Father of his Country," who passed with his troops within sight of the old mansion on his march to the West during the Braddock war. Here, too, is where Tarleton stopped with a portion of his troops in 1781, when upon his raid to Charlottesville, in a vain attempt to capture Governor Jefferson and the

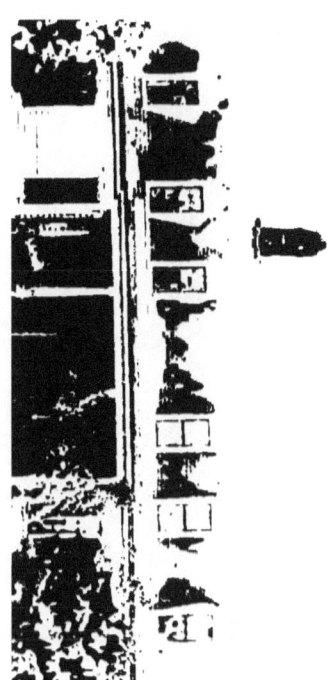

SOUTH-WEST MOUNTAINS

Legislature, but was detained at Castle Hill by a very tardy but sumptuous breakfast. It is said that the British general became quite irate at the delay in serving the meal, and stalked into the kitchen demanding the cause, whereupon that worthy functionary, the colored cook, said, "De soldiers dun eat up two breakfuses as fast as I kin cook 'em." The general then ordered the men to be flogged, being first tied to a cherry-tree, the site of which is still shown, and were most unmercifully whipped, their loud cries resounding over the place. This delay, however, was the means of saving the governor, as a messenger had been quickly despatched to notify him of the advancing enemy. The spot where once stood the ox-heart cherry-tree referred to is where Dr. Walker would frequently meet and parley with the Indian chiefs on their way to Williamsburg, an interesting account of which is to be found in the "Genealogy of the Page Family of Virginia," by Dr. R. C. M. Page, of New York, who also gives a history of the Walker family. If we trace back the "Walkers," who have been prominent in Colonial history from 1709, we will find that Dr. Thomas Walker, who was born 1715, was the fourth in descent from Thomas Walker, of Gloucester County, first of the family in Virginia, who was a member of the Colonial Assembly, 1662.

The English Walkers, from whom are directly descended the Virginia family, were of the nobility, many being particularly mentioned in early English history. They were quite prominent in the Established Church, as we read of the eminent Rev. Dr. Samuel Walker, grandson of Sir Thomas Walker, who represented the city of Exeter in many successive Parliaments during the reigns of Charles I. and II. He married the only daughter of the Rev. S. Hall, youngest son of the venerable Bishop Hall, a prelate to whom he was related by bonds more binding than those of consanguinity.

Sir Thomas Walker was born at Exeter, 1714. From him descended Robert Walker, of Kingston, who emigrated from Scotland to Virginia with two brothers, who respectively settled in Brunswick and Albemarle Counties some time before the Revolution. One of these brothers was the first Thomas Walker referred to above. The English Walkers are described as being "tall and of pleasing countenance and general deportment, such as to command great respect; grave and dignified, but always affable and cheerful in intercourse with others." These characteristics seem to be strikingly inherited by their Virginia descendants.

By the marriage of Dr. Walker, in 1741, with Mildred Thornton, widow of Nicholas Meriwether (3d), he came into possession of nearly one-half of the Meriwether lands along the South-West Mountains, the other half going to Colonel Robert Lewis, of Belvoir, who had married Jane Meriwether, eldest daughter of Nicholas Meriwether (2d). Tradition says that Dr. Thomas Walker was the first white man to enter Kentucky, having gone there in 1750, thirteen years before Daniel

SOUTH-WEST MOUNTAINS

Boone. His hatchet, marked T. W., with which he blazed his trail, was afterwards found, and is still retained in the family. He was highly esteemed by and won the friendship of the principal tribes of Indians in the West, as well as the chief sachems in Virginia. He was present at the treaty of Lancaster, Pennsylvania, by which the colonists secured, in 1744, all the territory in Virginia as claimed by the Indians. Dr. Walker was also participant in a purchase of six millions of acres in 1777 from George Croghan, who had purchased it from the six united nations or tribes of Indians of this large body of land, which embraced nearly the whole of Ohio and Kentucky. Dr. Walker's part of this was an eighth of a forty-eighth part, and his two sons, John and Thomas, one-sixth and one-seventh part respectively. There are still held by the descendants deeds for several tracts of land in Albemarle as conveyed by Lord Dunmore, 1772, and also one of three hundred and fifty acres of land in Louisa County under patent granted by George III. Dr. Walker was a practising physician, and attended Colonel Peter Jefferson during his last sickness, a bill for which is still preserved. Perhaps there was no man who rendered more service to the colonists in preserving peace with the Indians and in gaining quiet possession of their lands than Dr. Thomas Walker, for which his intimacy with Washington and Jefferson proves the high estimation in which they held him.

The exact date of erection of the first building

at Castle Hill is not known. Dr. Walker built the present wooden part in 1764, but it was not quite completed even then. It fronted north-west, facing the mountain, which then formed the approach to the house, but when the brick addition was made in 1824 by Hon. William C. Rives, the front was changed to the south-east, as at present.

Dr. Walker by his first marriage with Mildred Thornton Meriwether had twelve children. To his eldest son, John, was given the Belvoir tract. Mary Walker married Nicholas Lewis, of The Farm, near Charlottesville; Susan married Henry Fry, of Albemarle; Thomas Walker, Jr., married Margaret Hoopes, and settled at Indian Fields; Lucy Walker married Dr. George Gilmer, of Pen Park, near Charlottesville; Elizabeth married the Rev. Matthew Maury, second pastor of old Walker's Church; Mildred married Joseph Horsby, of Williamsburg, Virginia; Sarah married Colonel Reuben Lindsay, of Albemarle; Martha married George Divers, of Farmington, Albemarle; Reuben died young; Francis Walker married Jane Byrd Nelson, of Yorktown, Virginia, and succeeded to the Castle Hill estate; Peachy Walker married Joshua Fry, of Kentucky.

The Hon. Francis Walker, who was born at Castle Hill, June 22, 1764, married the daughter of Colonel Hugh Nelson, of Yorktown, in 1798, and resided at Castle Hill until his death in 1806. He was very prominent in the political field, and represented the counties of Orange and Albemarle

SOUTH-WEST MOUNTAINS

in the United States Congress, 1793-95. His wife's sister, Maria Nelson, was one of the victims of the Richmond Theatre fire in 1811; her remains were identified by the Hon. Francis Walker's watch, which she wore on the fatal night, and which is now in possession of Dr. Robert W. Nelson, of Charlottesville, Virginia. By the union of Francis Walker and Jane Nelson there were three children: Jane Frances Walker, the eldest, was born in the celebrated Nelson House, at Yorktown, Virginia; she married Dr. Mann Page in 1815, who, with his wife, moved to Turkey Hill, a part of the Castle Hill estate. Thomas Hugh Walker, the only son of Francis Walker, died when five years old; the second daughter and third child, Judith Page Walker, was born at Castle Hill in 1802; she married, March 24, 1819, the Hon. William C. Rives, United States Senator from Virginia. Mrs. Rives died at Castle Hill, June 23, 1882, at the age of eighty years, having survived her husband fourteen years. Mr. Rives was one of the most prominent statesmen of his day, and gave a lustre to diplomacy, both at home and abroad, such as has not been equalled since. In 1809-11 he studied law under Thomas Jefferson; 1814-15, was aide-de-camp to General John H. Cocke, of Virginia; 1817-19, member of Virginia House of Delegates from Nelson County, and in 1822-23 the same for Albemarle County; 1823-29, a Representative in the United States Congress; 1829-32, United States minister to France; 1832-45, United States Senator from Virginia; 1849–53, again United States minister to France, after which he retired to private life, and spent his remaining years at Castle Hill, where he prepared his " History of the Life and Times of James Madison," a work which for historic interest and beauty of language stands complete. The last public act of Mr. Rives was as a delegate to the " Peace Conference" in February, 1861, where he raised his voice against the hasty secession of Virginia, in an earnest effort to save the rupture of a Union which he loved so well and had served so long and faithfully. No courtier of the eighteenth century could surpass Mr. Rives in elegance of manner and graceful speech; he carried this even into the daily walks of life, and would converse with a child with as much courtesy as to a statesman. He possessed a most musical voice, and whenever he read the service at old Walker's Church, which he frequently did in the absence of a preacher, his clear, ringing tones and impressive manner rendered it most pleasing to his hearers. As an orator and writer he stood foremost among the *literati* of the day; none who ever heard him can forget his wonderful force of argument, clothed in chaste and beautiful language; too polite to attack his opponent with vituperative epithets while on the hustings, he would win the applause of even his bitterest political foes by his graceful and facetious expressions in opposing debate.

At the age of seventy-five Mr. Rives passed away, his county, State, and country at large losing a citizen who for brilliancy of mind, shrewdness in diplo-

SOUTH-WEST MOUNTAINS

macy, and force of character has scarcely been equalled. In the name of William Cabell Rives we find another noble family of Virginia, that of Cabell; this is for his mother, who was the daughter of the celebrated Dr. William Cabell, whose father, also Dr. William Cabell, first of the family, was surgeon in the British navy, and settled in Virginia somewhere about 1720 or 1725. It is said he owned twenty-five thousand acres of land on James River, in the counties of Nelson and Amherst.

The Cabells have always been highly distinguished for their learning, having held many important positions in the State. Dr. William Cabell, Jr., represented his district in Congress. He died upon his fine estate, Union Hill, in Nelson County, the mansion of which is said to have resembled Mount Vernon in appearance, though it was much larger. Mrs. William C. Rives was none the less prominent as a Virginia matron; by her gentle grace of manner and winning conversational powers she gave a charm to the Castle Hill circle which has not been since seen. She possessed a fluent, gifted pen, from which emanated several works, one a charming Virginia story, "Home and the World," and an "Epitome of the Bible" for children. Her efforts were all for "doing good" to those around her and to ameliorate the hardships of life to those less fortunate. Her great life-work was the erection and support of the handsome Gothic stone church which stands in sight of the old homestead; for this she devoted many years of patient labor, exerting her pen in touching appeals, that this "House of God" might be completed according to her original design, which was a great innovation upon the rude structures called "churches" of that day. It now stands complete, a lasting monument to her pious zeal and a blessing to many future generations.

The children of Mr. and Mrs. William C. Rives are:

1. Hon. Francis Robert Rives, of New York. He was secretary of the United States Legation at London under Hon. Edward Everett as minister, 1842–45. He married, in 1848, Matilda Antonia Barclay, of New York City. Their six children are: George Lockhart Rives; married, first, Caroline Kean, of New Jersey, 1873; second, Mrs. Belmont, of New York. Ella Louisa Rives; married David King, Jr., of Newport, Rhode Island, 1875. Francis Robert Rives, Jr.; married Georgia Fellows, of New York, 1879. Constance Rives; married Mr. Borland. Maud Rives; married Walker Breese Smith, of New York, 1882. Reginald William Rives; married, and has issue.

2. William Cabell Rives, Jr., of Newport, Rhode Island; born 1825; died 1890. He married, 1849, Grace Winthrop Sears, of Boston, Massachusetts. Their three children are: Dr. William C. Rives, of New York City; married, in 1876, Mary F. Rhinelander, of New York. Alice Rives; died single. Arthur Landon Rives; not married. David Sears, Esq., of Boston, Massachusetts, the father of Mrs. Grace Rives, gave the fine bell of Grace Church, Albemarle, Virginia, which weighs fifteen hundred and seventy-five pounds, and was cast by Mr. Hooper, of Boston, in 1855. Though the church was destroyed by fire in 1894, yet this bell, which fell more than fifty feet from the lofty tower, was uninjured, and still rings forth its clear tones each Sabbath.

SOUTH-WEST MOUNTAINS

3. Colonel Alfred Landon Rives; born at Castle Hill, 1830. He married, in 1859, Sadie McMurdo, daughter of James B. McMurdo, of Richmond, Virginia. Their three children are: Amélie Louise Rives, the authoress; married, first, John Armstrong Chanler, of New York; second, Prince Pierre Troubetzkoy, 1895. Gertrude Rives; married Allen Potts, of Richmond, Virginia, 1896. Sarah Landon Rives. Colonel Alfred L. Rives graduated with high honors at the Paris *École des Ponts et Chaussées*, 1850. He assisted General Meigs as architect in the construction of the new Capitol wing at Washington, 1859-60. Also architect of Cabin John's Bridge near Washington, D.C., being one of the longest single stone arches in the country. He served as chief of military engineers in the Confederate army with the rank of colonel. Since the war he has had charge of the civil engineer department on the Panama Canal until 1894, from which time he has resided at the ancestral home, Castle Hill, which he now owns.

4. Amélie Louise Rives was born at Paris, July 8, 1832. She was named for the wife of Louis Philippe, who was a great friend of the family. She was educated at the school of Mrs. A. M. Mead, Richmond, Virginia, and also studied in Paris in 1850. In 1854 she married Henry Sigourney, of Boston, Massachusetts. She and her husband with their three youngest children were lost at sea by the sinking of the "Ville du Havre," November 22, 1873. Their only surviving child, Henry Sigourney, Jr., is now of Boston, Massachusetts. There were few women in this country more gifted with love of art, music, and literature than Mrs. Sigourney. As an artist she stood above the ordinary ranks, as specimens of her brush testify. As a musician she was pronounced by her teacher, the celebrated Meyerbeer, as beyond his instruction. As a linguist in the ancient and modern languages, Professor George S. Hale, of Boston, her teacher, said she went far ahead of any female in this

country. And for beauty the great artist Guillaume pronounced her to possess the most perfect form and features that had ever sat to him.

5. Ella Rives was the youngest of the Hon. William C. Rives's daughters. She with her sister visited France in 1849, and enjoyed the high advantages of the foreign schools. She never married, but lived most of the time at Castle Hill, striving with her mother to smooth the rough path of life to the surrounding poor. In after-years she built a beautiful little villa, Beau Val, on a portion of the Castle Hill estate, near Cobham Station, and there lived for a time, to make happy those whom she had befriended. She died in 1891, her grave being marked by a massive cross in the Grace Church cemetery.

Readers of contemporary literature will readily recall the brilliant entry into the world of letters made by the Princess Troubetzkoy some ten or fifteen years ago. As Amélie Rives she scored an almost instant success by the publication of her first story, "A Brother to Dragons." This exquisite little bit of fiction, appearing under the distinguished chaperonage of the *Atlantic Monthly*, caught the popular fancy at once, and literary critics everywhere proclaimed the advent of a new and brilliant star in the Southern heavens, a fit addition to the rare constellation already glowing there. In rather quick succession followed her other works,—"The Farrier Lass O' Piping Pebworth," "Virginia of Virginia," "Nurse Crumpet Tells the Story," "Herod and Mariamne," "The Quick or the Dead?" "Asmodeus," "Athelwold," "The Witness of the Sun," "Barbara Dering," "According to St. John," "Tanis the Sang Digger," and recently "A Damsel Errant," besides a number of short stories and poems. Of all these none so increased her fame as "The Quick or the Dead?" published by the Lippincotts, a story of intense word-painting, such unconventional freedom, and so pronounced in its realism that it instantly became the sensation of the hour. Its publication brought forth a torrent of criticism, and while much of this was adverse in its tenor, the fame of the daring young authoress spread all the more, and the presses, "working day and night, could not possibly supply the demand."

Perhaps her next most famous work was "Herod and Mariamne," wholly different in theme, and incomparably superior to "The Quick or the Dead?" It is a drama of wonderful strength and rare brilliancy for one so young, and is undoubtedly the very flower of her genius. "Athelwold," while not so ambitious an effort as its predecessor, is also a drama of great talent, and makes the reader wonder why its fair creator should ever quit this especial field in which her genius seems to excel. As an example of simple touching pathos, "Virginia of Virginia" has few equals in Southern literature; while "The Farrier Lass O' Piping Pebworth" and, indeed, many of its associates, are richly gemmed with similes of extreme beauty and appropriateness. Her latest book, "A Damsel Errant," also published by the Lippincotts, is still another departure from the author's previous methods, being a romance of mediæval France.

Princess Troubetzkoy still writes for the magazines and is still popular with their readers. If she has some adverse critics she also has many warm admirers, and these latter must ever delight to dwell upon the various attributes of her genius, her great talent for vivid word-painting, her artistic value of perspective, her accurate setting of historic incidents, her wonderful intuitive powers of perception, and the innate nobility of her ideals.

Castle Hill still sits in calm repose, clothed with its intensely interesting associations and traditions, when its halls would be filled with many distinguished gatherings of the loved, the gifted, and the noble of our land, as well as from foreign shores. Here true beauty and grace were wont to be displayed; here the poetry of song with the charm of social intercourse heard; here every tree and shrub are linked with hallowed associations, where 'neath waving boughs and winding walks the noble countenance and handsome form of Presidents, statesmen, generals, authors, scientists, and divines have been seen; all make this historic old spot a real Mecca, where the lover of true genius and noble worth can worship.

We rejoice that Castle Hill has been so sacredly preserved with all its original surroundings. It stands like a monument to mark the connecting link between the past, with all its stirring heroic events of the infant colony, and the present age of wonderful advance in architecture, science, and art, and as the years roll on it will become ineffaceably dear to the heart of the most remote family descendant as well as to every Virginian.

KESWICK

THE HOME OF THE PAGES

NEXT to Castle Hill on the north-east comes the Keswick plantation, being that portion of the Walker tract as given by Hon. Francis Walker, of Castle Hill, to his eldest daughter, Jane Frances Walker, who married Dr. Mann Page. This farm is separated from that of Castle Hill by the public road, which crosses the mountain at Turkey Sag gap, which was once much travelled, but since has fallen into disuse and is almost impassable. Keswick farm was formerly called Turkey Hill, probably from the name of the gap, or the number of wild turkeys there always found; but after the settlement here by Dr. Page it was named Keswick, doubtless for the home of the poet Southey in Cumberland County, England, which sits at the foot of the Skiddaw Mountain, which rises on its north side; this present Keswick has also a high mountain (Peter's) to the north, while the mansion is surrounded by undulating hills on each side which screen it from view until the summit of these hills is reached, when it breaks upon the approaching visitor, seated in the beautiful valley below.

The old Turkey Hill plantation contained originally three thousand seven hundred acres of the

Walker's tract, extending from the summit of Peter's Mountain nearly to the Louisa line. The house, which at first was quite small, sits upon a gently sloping hill crowned with a dense growth of oaks and locust-trees. The lawn is extensive and covered with waving grass, while at the foot of the hill bubbles a sparkling spring of never-failing water, which has been used for several generations, the water being "toted" up the hill by the numerous blacks. The first house of any consequence was built by Dr. Page about the year 1818. It consisted simply of a double log house of four rooms; afterwards this was plastered and weather-boarded, making an exceedingly warm and comfortable house. In 1832 the front or frame part as now seen was added, being one story and a half high, with a wide centre hall. In 1849–50 this again was remodelled and improved, as shown in the cut. The front rooms are spacious and quite out of proportion to those above, which in buildings of that day were quite small, but served the family quite amply as sleeping apartments. Much of the furniture of the present house is antique, some having been brought from England at an early period; among which is still standing the family clock, brought over by Dr. Thomas Walker, which continues to mark the time with accuracy, though the rawhide strings of its massive weights have never been removed, and is perhaps the best preserved "grandfather's" clock in the country. The Pages still keep sacred many relics of their ancient and noble family, which can

SOUTH-WEST MOUNTAINS

here be seen, such as books, papers, and documents musty with age, which bear the handwriting of kings, governors, Presidents, Indian chiefs, and a host of eminent statesmen and men of profession. Adjoining the lawn is a large garden, in one portion of which was once the family burying-ground, but which has been removed to the Grace Church cemetery, where the graves are marked by handsome stones.

"The Genealogy of the Page Family," as given by R. C. M. Page, of New York, presents a most complete and interesting account of this famous family, to which we refer the reader more particularly. We will give, however, a brief extract from it, showing the direct descent of the "Keswick" Page family.

Colonel John Page, first of the family in Virginia, was the son of Francis Page, of Middlesex County, England. He came to Virginia, and settled at Williamsburg about 1650. He died in 1692; his tombstone, with inscription, is still to be seen in the old graveyard at Williamsburg, Virginia. He was "One of His Majesties' Council in the Dominion of Virginia," and was very prominent in its early governance. Colonel John Page married Alice Luckin, also of England; they had two sons, Francis and Matthew, both born at Williamsburg, Virginia. Captain Francis Page was clerk of the House of Burgesses, 1688. He married Mary Diggs, daughter of Edward Diggs, of Hampton, Virginia; they had but one child, a daughter, who married John Page, a lawyer, and died without children. The second son of Colonel John Page, Matthew Page, settled at Rosewell, Gloucester County, Virginia. He was called "Honorable Collonell Mathew Page, Esq.," who was one of His Majesty's Council in Virginia, and died 1703. He married Mary Mann, daughter of John Mann, of Gloucester County, Virginia. They had four children, three of whom died young; the surviving son, Mann Page, was a member of the Colonial Council under George I., and built the celebrated mansion Rosewell, on the York River. He died in 1730. He married, first, Judith Wormley, daughter of Hon. Ralph Wormley, secretary of the colony; second, Judith Carter, daughter of the celebrated Robert Carter, commonly called "King Carter," of Crotoman, Lancaster County. By his first marriage were three children, only one of which left issue, Maria, who was the grandmother of Governor Mann Randolph, of Edgehill. By his second wife, Judith Carter, were six children. The second son, John Page, was born at Rosewell, 1720; he married Jane Bird, of Westover, James River, 1746, and died 1780; he was also one of the Virginia Council. They had fifteen children, eleven of whom married and settled in different parts of the State. His fourth son and sixth child, Carter Page, was born 1758; he removed to Willis' Fork, Cumberland County, Virginia, where he settled in 1783. He married, first, Mary Carey, and second, Lucy, daughter of Governor Thomas Nelson, of Yorktown, Virginia, in 1799. He served as major in the Revolutionary war, and was aide-de-camp to General Lafayette; he was also one of the committee to receive him when on his visit to Richmond, Virginia. He died in 1825.

From his first marriage there were eight children; his fifth son and sixth child was Dr. Mann Page, of Keswick, who was born at the "Fork," October 26, 1791. He married Jane Frances Walker, of Castle Hill, on December 12, 1815; the marriage taking place in Richmond, Virginia, at the old Virginia Tavern, which faced the Capitol Square, opposite St. Paul's Church, and was then the swell hotel of the city, which was kept by Mrs. Colonel Hugh Nelson, her maternal grandmother. The old tavern afterwards passed into the hands of Captain Thomas Nelson until he removed from the city.

The daughter of Mrs. Hugh Nelson, Maria, lost her life in the burning of the Richmond Theatre in 1811, the fire being distinctly seen from the Virginia Tavern, several of whose guests were also victims.

Dr. Page graduated at Hampden-Sidney College, and also at the Medical College at Philadelphia, in 1813. He practised medicine for a while in Richmond, until his marriage, when he removed to his wife's estate in Albemarle County. Dr. Page was one of the distinguished citizens of the county, who sat with General Lafayette at the dinner given him in 1824 by the citizens of Albemarle at the University of Virginia, and his name appears in connection with that of Hon. William C. Rives in many of the church records, showing him to have been a zealous supporter of the church.

Dr. Page did not enter very largely into the practice of his profession while in the county, not wishing to intrude upon that of his wife's kinsman, Dr. Thomas Meriwether, but preferred the cultivation of his large and profitable farm. He was a man of commanding stature, having a kind, benevolent countenance, and most entertaining in conversation. He died and was buried at Keswick, May 15, 1850.

Jane Frances Walker, his wife, was, like her sister Judith, quite brilliant in mind, but possessed an extremely reserved and gentle disposition, thus exhibiting more plainly the traits of her Nelson kin, being much like her mother, Jane Byrd Nelson, both in appearance and manner. She died February 7, 1873, having survived her husband twenty-three years.

By the union of Dr. Mann Page and Jane Frances Walker were twelve children:

1. Maria Page; died unmarried.
2. Ella Page; lived to be sixty-four years of age and died single.
3. Francis Walker Page, eldest son; born 1820; died 1846; married Anna E., daughter of Benjamin F. Cheeseman, of New York, leaving one son, Frank Walker Page, now professor of music at Staunton, Virginia.
4. Carter Henry Page; born 1822; married Leila, daughter of Captain William Graham, of Baltimore, Maryland. Their children are: Leila G. Page, born 1858; died 1894. William Graham Page; born 1860. Is a lawyer of Charlottesville, Virginia. Carter H. Page, Jr.; born 1864; civil engineer of

SOUTH-WEST MOUNTAINS

   Philadelphia. Mary Bowdin Page; born 1866; married Mr. Gilbert Bird, of England.
5. John Cary Page; born 1824; died 1826.
6. Frederick Winslow Page; born 1826; now librarian of the University of Virginia; married, first, Anne Kinloch, daughter of Dr. Thomas Meriwether, of Kinloch, and great-granddaughter of Governor Thomas Nelson, of Yorktown, Virginia. They had seven children: Jane Walker; born 1851; married Thomas W. Lewis, of Castalia. Eliza M.; born 1853; died single, 1873. Annie Nelson; born 1855; married, 1875, Nat Coleman, of Halifax County, Virginia. Frederick K.; born 1857; married Flora Lewis, of Albemarle, Virginia. William Douglas; born 1859; died 1878. Evelyn Byrd; born 1862; married John Coleman, of Halifax County, Virginia. Mildred Nelson; born 1865; resides in New York.
7. Jane Walker Page; died unmarried, 1845, aged seventeen. She was quite talented.
8. Mann Page, Jr.; married Mary Ann Hobson, of Powhatan County, Virginia. They lived on a part of Keswick farm, near the mountain; he was a fine scholar and taught at the Keswick School, 1849. He died 1864, leaving one daughter, Charlotte Nelson Page.
9. Charlotte Nelson Page; born at Turkey Hill, 1832; died at Kinloch, of typhoid fever, 1844, unmarried. She was like her sister, Jane Walker, very bright in mind. She attended Mrs. A. M. Mead's school in Richmond with her cousins Amélie and Ella Rives, of Castle Hill.
10. William Wilmer Page; born 1835; died 1857, aged twenty-two.
11. Thomas Walker Page; born April 18, 1837; died 5th of June, 1887, aged fifty. Married, in 1861, Nannie Watson, daughter of James Morris, of Sylvania, Green Springs, Louisa County, Virginia. He succeeded to the homestead after the death of his

mother in 1873. He, like his father, was very active in the church, and for many years was warden and treasurer of Grace Church. The children of Thomas Walker Page are Ella Rives Page, born in 1862; James Morris Page, A.M. and Ph.D. of Leipsic, Germany; born 1864; principal of the Keswick School, now professor of mathematics at the University of Virginia. Thomas Walker Page, Jr., A.M., assistant principal of Keswick School. Constance Morris Page; born 1869. Mann Page; born 1871. Susan Morris Page; born 1878.

12. Dr. Richard Channing Moore Page, last child and eighth son of Dr. Mann Page, was born 2d of January, 1841, at Turkey Hill. Removed to New York City in 1867; married, in 1874, Mrs. Elizabeth Fitch, widow of the Hon. Richard Henry Winslow, of New York. Dr. Page is quite eminent as a physician and has a lucrative practice in New York City. He is quite literary, and is the author of the "Genealogy of the Page Family," which embraces that also of the Walker, Nelson, Pendleton, and Randolph families. Other writings upon medical and scientific subjects have emanated from his pen. He has spent much time in Europe, is fond of the arts, and has adorned his beautiful residence in New York with some of the choicest paintings of the old masters, the beauty of which is only exceeded by that of his charities and liberality to those around him. He has no children. Since writing the above, the death of Dr. Channing Page has been announced in the New York papers.

It will be observed that there has been a *Mann* Page in nearly every branch of the family from the first Mann Page, of Rosewell, on the York, 1691, son of Hon. Matthew Page and Mary Mann, who was an heiress, born 1672, and died 1707; from her the name of Mann descended.

SOUTH-WEST MOUNTAINS

The widow of Thomas W. Page now resides at the Keswick farm.

There has always been a school at Keswick for boys. Dr. Mann Page from the first spared no expense in procuring the best teachers for the home education of his children, and when grown, in sending them to the best colleges that the State afforded. All of his six sons were highly educated and fitted for life. We extract from the " Page" book the following interesting synopsis of the schools held at the homestead or near by, as it records the names of prominent men now living. One thing to be noted of the Keswick School was its bounteous table, which always groaned with the abundance of the farm; the boys were always kept fat, and its luxurious living added to the watchful, tender care of its generous mistress, Mrs. Jane Page, made Keswick always an attractive place for them, and from which they would leave with great reluctance.

The first school as recorded is that of—

" 1831-32.—William W. Hawkins taught for a short time at the old Bentivoglio Tavern, which was kept at that time by Joseph W. Campbell. The school was then removed to a log house in the woods near by, called the ' Tick Hill Academy.' Among the pupils were Frank W. Page, Carter H. Page, James Farish and John T. Farish (twin-brothers), Reuben Gordon, William F. Gordon, Jr., Lewis Miller, and others. Mr. John T. Farish died in New York a few years ago a millionaire. The old Bentivoglio Tavern, called ' Old Benti' for short, stood on the south side of the public road, about a quarter of a mile east of the mouth of the Turkey Sag. The latter is the name of the public road that runs north-west over the mountains, along Feather-Bed Lane, across Turkey Run, and through Turkey Gap. The tavern was originally built by Hon. Francis Walker, of Castle Hill, for the accommodation of travellers in those days. It has long since gone to ruin, and nothing but a depression in the ground now remains to mark the original site. The post-office at Lindsay's turnout on the railroad, some two miles distant, is known as Bentivoglio. This and other beautiful Italian names for places in the neighborhood, such as Modina and Monticello, were doubtless given by Italian laborers imported in early times by Thomas Jefferson for the purpose of introducing grape-culture."

This is a mistake; Mr. Jefferson named Monticello himself. Many of his Italian laborers, however, whose descendants are still among us, did give names to their homes, such as *Colle*, *Porto Bello*, and *Bentivoglio*.

"1832–33.—Mr. Crawford taught at the same place with the same scholars. Crawford was an exhorter in the Baptist Church and used the hickory freely. The boys were much afraid of him. Sometimes he would be absent the whole day preaching and the boys would be afraid to go home. In the evening he would return, and the whole school be drawn up in line in the public road and put through a course of spelling.

SOUTH-WEST MOUNTAINS

"1833-34.—James L. Gordon taught at Edgeworth, the residence of his father, General William F. Gordon, with much the same scholars.

"1834-35.—William W. Hawkins rented Bentivoglio Tavern and taught school again, Mr. Campbell having left. The scholars were nearly the same.

"1835-36.—Mr. Provost, a graduate of Princeton, New Jersey, taught at Castle Hill, the residence of Hon. William C. Rives. There were a limited number of pupils, among whom were Frank W. Page, Carter H. Page, Frederick W. Page, Francis R. Rives, and William C. Rives, Jr. Provost was one of the best teachers. He also courted all the marriageable girls in the neighborhood.

"1836-37.—Edwin Hall, of Maine, a pupil of the poet Longfellow and a graduate of Bowdoin, taught at Bentivoglio. Among the pupils were Frank W. Page, Carter H. Page, Frederick W. Page, Reuben Gordon, William Gordon, Henry Miclin, Johnson Miclin, and Lewis Miller.

"1837-38.—Giles Waldo, a graduate of Yale, taught at Bentivoglio. The scholars were the same, with the addition of William Anderson and Richard Anderson, of Richmond, Virginia, as boarders.

"1838-39.—Mr. Janes, of Burlington, Vermont, taught at Bentivoglio. Among the scholars were Robert W. Nelson, W. Douglas Meriwether, William C. Rives, Jr., Lewis Miller, William Lewis (colonel), the brothers William, Richard, and Jack Anderson, Carter and Frederick Page.

"1839-40.—Jacob Belville, of Princeton, taught at Bentivoglio with the same pupils, except R. W. Nelson, William and Richard Anderson.

"1840-41-42.—James Chisholm, of Harvard, taught at Keswick in the old school-house down in the lot. Among the scholars were Frederick W. Page, Mann Page, Jr., Wilmer Page, Lindsay Walker, George and Charles Gordon (twin-brothers), Alexander Gordon, and Alfred Rives.

"1842-43.—Thomas W. Cattell, of New Jersey, graduate of Princeton, taught at the same place. The scholars were Frederick Mann, Wilmer and Tom Page, George, Charles Churchill, and Alexander Gordon, and William C. Cattell.

"1843-44.—George Jeffery, of Cambridge, England, taught at the same place, with the same scholars, except Frederick W. Page. It was about this time that F. W. Meerbach, a famous German pianist, gave music lessons to young ladies in the neighborhood. Mr. Jeffery was a very eccentric man, and the two had a quarrel, resulting in Mr. Jeffery going next session to Edgeworth."

We may further add that the above German, Meerbach, was a music teacher in Mrs. A. M. Mead's large seminary in Richmond, and was recommended by her to Dr. Page. He was very irritable, and got into several fracases in Richmond. The "eccentric Jeffery" we have already spoken of in our article on Cismont.

"1844-45.—George Jeffery at Edgeworth, the residence of General Gordon; the same boys except William C. Cattell.

SOUTH-WEST MOUNTAINS

"1845-46.—Mr. Taylor, a Princeton man, taught at Edgeworth with the same scholars.

"1846-47-48.—Frederick W. Page taught at Keswick, in the old school-house in the lot. The scholars were Frank Hopkins Churchill and Alexander Gordon, Mann, Wilmer, Thomas, and Channing Page. The latter wore a check apron, much to his annoyance.

"1848-49.—Calvin S. Maupin, of North Carolina, taught at Edgeworth, with the same boys except Channing, who was too young to walk there. Mr. Maupin was not a very literary man, nor did he much enjoy conversation at meals, being usually blessed with a ravenous appetite. Thus, while General Gordon was telling some anecdote about President Jackson while he was a member of Congress, Mr. Maupin interrupted him in the middle of the most interesting part by remarking, 'General, you got my bread!'

"1849-50.—Mann Page taught at Keswick. The scholars were Churchill, Alexander, and Mason Gordon, Henry Lewis, Wilmer, Thomas, Channing Page, and Edward C. Mead, who was then living at Cismont.

"1850-51.—Dabney T. C. Davis taught at Keswick. He was a graduate of the University of Virginia. The scholars were John and Hugh Nelson, twin-brothers and boarders, Wilmer, Thomas, and Channing Page, Churchill, Alexander, and Mason Gordon, John and Rice McGee, also twin-brothers.

"1851-52.—Samuel S. Carr, of the University of

Virginia, taught at Keswick. The scholars were the same except Churchill Gordon. Lewis McGee, brother of John and Rice, was a scholar this year. They came from Bedford County, and boarded at Logan, the residence of Captain M. Lewis Walker."

After this the school was discontinued at Keswick until about the year 1887, when it was revived by Dr. James M. Page, assisted by his brother, Thomas W. Page, Jr. They enlarged and added several buildings for boarders, and under the name of Keswick School it attained quite a celebrity, numbering some thirty pupils. Dr. James Page has since been made professor of mathematics at the University of Virginia. After the discontinuance of the school, Thomas W. Page, Jr., went to Europe, graduating at Leipsic, Germany, with high honors, having taken the degree of Doctor of Philosophy, *summa cum laude*, which is rarely accomplished. Dr. Thomas Page was engaged for some time, while in London, collecting material for a book concerning the relations of "Work and Wages in England immediately after the Period of the Black Death." Since his return to this country he has been appointed professor in the University of California.

EDGEWORTH

THE HOME OF THE GORDONS

IN 1755, Dr. Thomas Walker, of Castle Hill, sold or gave about four hundred acres of his land as a glebe for the churches then established at Walker's in Albemarle, Trinity in Louisa, and one in Orange County. This glebe tract joined the lands of Captain James Lindsay, and it is believed that most of the land purchased for this purpose was from him, the remainder being given by Dr. Walker, whose daughter had married Rev. Matthew Maury, son of the first pastor of Walker's Church, who lived here until his death in 1808.

Upon this tract, which altogether contained nearly one thousand acres, was built a parsonage by the several vestries, with all necessary out-buildings, which, we may presume, were at that day nothing more than rude log cabins erected in the wild forest.

Here the Rev. James Maury, the first pastor of the three churches, lived. He was quite a prominent and able man during his day, preaching for a large circuit in the surrounding counties, and also teaching a small school located near his residence, to which Jefferson, Madison, and Monroe attended when boys, besides others who afterwards became distinguished men. He was quite learned in the classics, as young Jefferson wrote to his school-boy friend Governor John Page that he was a " fine scholar," and evidently he left his impress upon these young minds, to which they owed much of their success in after-life. The old log school-house in which he taught stood in one corner of the Edgeworth yard, the site of which is now marked by a hedge of cedars. The Rev. James Maury married a Miss Walker, supposed to have been a cousin of Dr. Walker, through whose influence he became rector of the parish. Mr. Maury had a family of ten children, most of whom married and scattered over the State, their descendants filling many high and honored positions. He died in 1769, and was buried under the pulpit of old Walker's Church, where he had so faithfully preached for many years. There now stands a monument in front of the present Grace Church, erected to his memory, marking the spot where once stood the old Colonial church, with the following inscription:

> " Sacred to the memory
> of
> REV. JAMES MAURY,
> First Pastor of Walker's Parish.
> Born April 8th, 1717;
> Died June 9th, 1769.
> This monument was erected by Elizabeth Walker as a tribute to his Piety, Learning, and Worth."

He was succeeded by his eldest son, Rev. Matthew Maury, who lived at the glebe, and taught in the same log school-house as his father. He married, in 1773, Elizabeth Walker (called

SOUTH-WEST MOUNTAINS

Betsy), fourth daughter of Dr. Thomas Walker. From him descended the Hon. Matthew F. Maury, the "Pathfinder of the Seas," whose memory all nations delight to honor. It was not far from the glebe that the Rev. James Waddell, the blind preacher, lived, who was made famous by William Wirt. Both of these ministers were quite intimate, and when the wife of Mr. Maury died he invited Mr. Waddell to preach her funeral sermon, there being no Episcopal minister beside himself in the county and but few at that time in the State.

The Rev. Mr. Waddell married Mary Gordon, the daughter of Colonel James Gordon. She was the sister of General William F. Gordon, who afterwards owned Edgeworth. By this marriage Mr. Waddell obtained a portion of the original Gordon tract, which embraced the town of Gordonsville, and which was named in honor of Colonel James Gordon, one of the Revolutionary heroes, who commanded one of the Virginia regiments at the surrender of Cornwallis at Yorktown, Virginia.

Rev. Mr. Waddell also taught a school near Gordonsville, at which Meriwether Clarke and Governor Barbour attended.

In 1802 the law authorizing the sale of the glebe lands throughout Virginia having passed, after the death of Mr. Maury, in 1808, the property was sold to a Mr. Ragland, and afterwards passed into the hands of General William F. Gordon, who moved there in 1835.

General Gordon occupied for a while the original frame house then standing, but which was soon after destroyed by fire, after which, about the year 1837, he built the present handsome brick structure, which is two stories in height, with double rooms and wide hall on each floor, besides a large cellar. It formed at that date an imposing building, being much superior to that of his neighbors, and its spacious apartments became the scene of a refined and elegant hospitality.

General Gordon was one of the foremost men of his day. He had served with great distinction in the war of 1812, and afterwards represented his county in the Virginia Legislature, and became Senator from Virginia in the United States Congress of 1829-35. In recognition of his able services he was tendered a public dinner in Amherst County, and had other honors bestowed upon him. General Gordon was always a stanch Whig and warmly sustained the election of Mr. Clay, but after that gentleman's defeat he retired from politics and devoted himself to his farm, making Edgeworth noted for its great productions. General Gordon was a fine speaker, most entertaining in conversation, having a fund of humor and anecdote gathered during a long and eventful political life, which made him *par excellence* a most agreeable companion. He always dressed quite plainly, and even while in Congress appeared in a suit of homespun made on his farm, to comport with the dress of his Southern Congressional brethren, who were furious at the passage of the Tariff law of 1827-28, and waved the flag of defiance to the Northern members by dressing in home-made cloth, eating their own hominy without the aid of Kentucky bacon, and walking rather than ride Western horses. General Gordon married Elizabeth Lindsay, the daughter of Colonel Reuben Lindsay, who also owned large landed possessions along the South-West Mountains. She was a woman of great intelligence, having much of the fire of her Scotch blood. She lived to the good old age of ninety-five, dying at the home of her youngest son, Mason Gordon, Esq., of Charlottesville, in 1886. The sister of Mrs. Gordon, Maria Lindsay, married Captain Meriwether Lewis Walker, son of "Dr. Tom" Walker, of Castle Hill, whose home, called Logan, after the Indian chief of that name, was situated but two miles from Edgeworth. Sarah Walker, another daughter of Dr. Walker, married, in 1778, Colonel Reuben Lindsay. She was his first wife. Their daughter, Sally Lindsay, married, in 1810, her first cousin, Captain James Lindsay, son of David Lindsay, who was a brother of Colonel Reuben Lindsay. This Captain Lindsay lived at the Meadows, another old homestead, which is now owned by Colonel John M. Patton, formerly of Richmond, Virginia. Captain Lindsay inherited all the lands of his father, which almost surrounded the Edgeworth farm, and extended even into Louisa County. Thus we see by the intermarriage of the Walkers, Lindsays, and Gordons these extensive lands were retained by their descendants for several generations, but which have since passed entirely out of those families. On the east side of

Edgeworth were the lands of Loudon Bruce, which extended to Gordonsville; he was famous for his fat cattle, which have supplied the markets so long.

By the marriage of General Gordon and Elizabeth Lindsay were ten children:

1. James Lindsay Gordon; married, first, Miss Beale; second, Miss Winston. They left no issue.
2. Reuben Lindsay Gordon; married Miss Beale, sister of the above. Had four daughters and two sons, Reuben L. and Alexander T.
3. William F. Gordon, Jr.; married Miss Morris. They had two sons and three daughters. His sons were William F. and James Morris.
4. George L. Gordon; now dead. He married Miss Daniel, of North Carolina. Had two sons, Armistead C. and James L. Gordon.
5. Charles H. Gordon, twin-brother of George; married, first, Miss Beale. Had one son, Professor James B. Gordon, who died in Arkansas, while professor of the Arkansas University. He was a most brilliant man. The second wife of Charles was Miss Boswell. No issue.
6. John Churchill Gordon; married Mary S. Pegram, daughter of Edward S. Pegram, of Albemarle, by whom he had six sons and three daughters. Dr. J. C. Gordon is now a practising physician of Charlottesville, Virginia.
7. Alexander Tazwell Gordon; married his cousin, Miss Gordon. Had one son and four daughters.
8. Mason Gordon; married Miss Hart, of North Carolina, by whom he had three sons and two daughters. His eldest daughter married Thomas L. Rosser, Jr., son of General Thomas L. Rosser, of Albemarle, who served in the Confederate army.
9. Maria Gordon.
10. Hannah Gordon; married, August 16, 1842, at Edgeworth, Judge William J. Robertson, of Charlottes-

ville, Virginia. Their children were: Elizabeth Lindsay, Lucy Gordon, Sally Brand, John McB., Maria Gordon (dead), Mary Carter, William Gordon, Nannie Morris (dead), and Reuben Lindsay.

All of the sons of General Gordon have been talented, and, like their father, brilliant orators, who have made their mark at the bar, among whom we may mention Mason Gordon, Esq., now a leading lawyer of Charlottesville, Virginia, and the grandson of General Gordon, the Hon. James L. Gordon (son of George L. Gordon), who is now of New York City, and has become a most noted public speaker both North and South.

As at Keswick, the home of Dr. Page, his near neighbor, so it was at Edgeworth, a school was always kept up, either at one place or the other, the boys of the two families forming quite a large school of themselves. The late Judge William J. Robertson, of Charlottesville, when a young man, taught for a while in the general's family, and while there fell in love with the pretty Hannah Gordon. The general opposed the match, principally on account of their youth, putting Mr. Robertson off with the promise of his daughter's hand when he was established at the bar. It was not long after when the general heard young Robertson make his maiden speech in a political contest at Louisa Court-House, and being so pleased with his effort that he removed all objections to the marriage, feeling satisfied that the future of the young man would be a brilliant one, which was verified, he becoming commonwealth's attorney in 1852 and judge of the Supreme Court of Virginia in 1859. He also practised in the Supreme Court of the United States, and was considered the most eminent of the State's judiciary.

After the death of General Gordon, Edgeworth was sold to Dr. Charles Hancock in 1858, who paid thirty-six thousand dollars for it. It was a magnificent estate at the time; its twelve hundred acres were divided into seven fields of one hundred acres each, besides more than five hundred acres of woodland stretching to the top of Peter's Mountain, while surrounding the house was an extensive garden and lawn of five acres. In 1859 Dr. Hancock greatly enlarged the mansion by a two-story frame addition to the rear of the brick front, thus forming an L in shape. The rooms in this fine building were twenty feet square, with wide centre hall, and proportionate in height, making it unapproachable by any country-seat in magnificent dimensions and beauty of finish. The farm also was in the highest state of production, often yielding fifteen hundred bushels of wheat from one field, one thousand barrels of corn, and forty thousand pounds of hay during one season; besides having twenty-three horses, twenty milch cows, and a vast herd of cattle. For several years Dr. Hancock cultivated this fine farm very extensively, expending large sums upon its improvement and for the production of large numbers of beef cattle for the Confederate army. After the war, about 1867, Edgeworth was sold to an Englishman named Russell, who accomplished very little with it, and who sold it to its present owner, a Mr. Edwards, who resides in England. It is said that this fine estate can now be bought for five dollars per acre! *O tempora! quid descendit!*

But we turn to contemplate the joyous home of Edgeworth as it was, with its jolly set of boys, always ready for a frolic, and its teachers as ready to join them, with books one day and dancing and fox-hunting the next; or let us look at its magnificent halls as filled by welcome guests, many of whom were the great men of the day, as they sit at the festive board and are entertained by the wit and humor of General Gordon. Such scenes were frequent, neighbors dropping in *sans cérémonie*, the girls and boys always welcomed by the "old folks" to have a good time, and thus it would continue a round of merriment throughout the year.

With Edgeworth we reach nearly the northeastern limit of the South-West Mountains of Albemarle, having traced the homes along its foot-hills on the eastern side; but we could continue these celebrated homesteads still farther, did space permit, even into Orange County, where sits at the extreme end of the mountain range the residence of James Barbour, one of Virginia's best governors; also that of John Taylor, son of "Old Zachary," who was celebrated for his intense Democracy, and, like Mr. Peter Meriwether, called every one a fool who did not believe in Mr. Jefferson; and then Richard Taliaferro just opposite, who married into the Gilmer family, whose name,

HISTORIC HOMES

from the Latin words *Talis Ferrum* (like iron), or the Italian *Tagliari-ferro* (to cut with iron), indicated the fighting stock of which he sprang, giving to Virginia some of her noblest warriors; but we now turn to those in Albemarle which sit along the old Machunk Creek, made famous by Indian legend, and which forms a part of this traditionary region.

COBHAM PARK

THE RESIDENCE OF THE LATE WILLIAM C. RIVES, JR.

ON an elevated plain, opposite Cobham Station, Chesapeake and Ohio Railroad, which courses at the foot of the South-West Mountains from Gordonsville to Charlottesville, sits a handsome residence, the top of which can but barely be seen from the railroad, so dense is the grove of forest-trees surrounding it. This is Cobham Park, the residence of the late William C. Rives, Jr., of Newport, Rhode Island, second son of Hon. William C. Rives, of Castle Hill. This lower portion of the Castle Hill plantation fell to him in the division of the estate, and here he built his beautiful summer residence about the year 1855. This original tract, which extends to the Louisa County line, contained more than one thousand acres, since which Mr. Rives has added several more tracts by purchase, and Cobham Park now contains two thousand four hundred acres. The greater portion of this large area is in original forests, which surround the house almost entirely, untouched of its gigantic trees. Mr. Rives was very tenacious of the noble oaks and pine upon his place, which he wished to retain, like the grand parks of England. It is said that such was his jealous care of them that he would frequently buy his firewood elsewhere rather than put the axe into his own woods. For the first few years after taking possession the farm was extensively cultivated, and large crops of corn, wheat, and tobacco were raised, but more for clearing the land than for the profit derived. Of late years the extensive fields surrounding the park have been kept in luxuriant grass, where herds of fine horses, cattle, and sheep are seen. Crossing a rustic bridge which spans the Machunk Creek, a park of about twenty acres is entered at the foot of a hill, up which the road gracefully winds, until the summit is reached, where entrance to the lawn proper is made. This park is studded with groups of oak, chestnut, poplar, ash, and every variety of forest-tree in all their magnificence, while between the hills course small rivulets and miniature cascades. The lawn itself, which embraces several acres, is filled with choice evergreens and shrubbery, which in summer give forth a fragrance and beauty truly refreshing. The mansion, which rises in stately proportions amid this wealth of luxuriant shade, is more modern in style than any of its neighbors. It is a handsome brick structure of nearly three stories, with wide portico, massive centre chimneys, and ornamental attic windows, from which a grand view of the entire range of mountains is obtained, stretching from Monticello to Peter's Mountain, a distance of fifteen miles. The wood-work of the house is highly finished, and was executed by McSparren, an Englishman, who had been brought from the North by Mrs.

William C. Rives, of Castle Hill, to complete the interior of Grace Church. He was a skilled architect and most superior workman, far above the ordinary mechanic in education. He was famous for using very high-sounding words in conversation, which would be given forth with a most pompous air, and proved quite mystifying to the illiterate. He constructed a spiral stairway to the upper stories of the Cobham mansion which he intended to be the *chef-d'œuvre* of his art; it appeared in its graceful curves to have no support, and Mrs. Rives suggested that it would not be safe; but McSparren, with a great flourish, assured her that a hogshead of tobacco might be rolled down the stairway " without the demolition of the least part, madam ;" yet Mrs. Rives insisted on having the lower portion closed up, much to his mortification; thus the spiral stair still stands with a closet underneath which conceals its fine proportions. His work was always full of graceful lines and very ornamental, which throughout the mansion is to be seen everywhere with pleasing effect. Its sixteen rooms are spacious and adorned with rich paintings, large mirrors, pendant chandeliers, antique oaken furniture, and all that could embellish and make complete a refined home. To the right of the mansion-house stands a large building containing bath- and office-rooms, with a conservatory adjoining, which is supplied with water by windmill-power. The outer buildings are upon the same complete order, which show taste and ornament in design as well as judicious care for the comfort of the stock, which is in sharp contrast to Virginia farming of the past.

Cobham Park takes its name from the little station on the Chesapeake and Ohio Railroad, which is seated a short distance from the foot of the hill upon which it sits. Cobham Station was named by the Hon. William C. Rives for the village of Cobham, in Surrey County, England. It sits upon a part of the Castle Hill tract, and when the railroad was completed from Gordonsville to this point in 1848, it was celebrated by a grand barbecue and speaking in honor of the first step taken towards the Ohio River. The writer of this can well remember that event, fraught with many circumstances which made a deep impression upon a young mind. The Hon. William C. Rives, then in his prime, and General Bankhead Magruder, fresh from the Mexican war, were the speakers. After the speaking there was a profusion of eating and drinking for the large crowd, and whiskey flowed freely, to the detriment of many. There had been, however, stowed away a few baskets of choice champagne for the distinguished speakers and guests, among whom was Colonel Fontaine, the president of the little "Virginia Central Railroad," with other officers and dignitaries. During the speaking, two wild chaps, Jim Gooch and Jim Leach, broke into the room and secured several bottles of the choice wine, and when Mr. Rives proposed the toasts for the occasion, the two boys flourished their bottles in the air, broke the necks and poured the wine down their capacious throats

SOUTH-WEST MOUNTAINS

much to the amusement of the crowd. A great many of the rough mountaineers came a long distance to see a locomotive for the first time, and when it sounded a shrill blast from its whistle the terrified farmers began a hasty retreat for their homes, fearing the " durned thing would bust."

William Cabell Rives, Jr., was born at Castle Hill in 1825. After graduating in the law at the University of Virginia he located at Newport, Rhode Island. In 1849 he married Grace Winthrop Sears, daughter of David Sears, Esq., a wealthy banker of Boston, Massachusetts. Their children are :

1. Dr. William C. Rives, of New York City, who married, in 1876, Mary F. Rhinelander, of New York.
2. Alice Rives, who died single.
3. Arthur Landon Rives, who lives with his mother.

Mr. Rives was taller in stature than his father, but possessed much of his grace and affability, which were always shown towards the most humble persons. He was most pleasant and attractive in conversation and a most eloquent speaker in public. In 1869 he delivered the oration before the Society of Alumni of the University of Virginia ; and, as his father had done before the strife of the nation began, so he, after the conflict was over, raised his voice in eloquent words to bring harmony and peace between the sections once more. He was a most liberal contributor to the little Grace Church, near his home, to which his ancestors have always been devoted. To his generous aid it owes its handsome rectory and grounds, also the extensive cemetery grounds surrounding the church. The beautiful marble tablets erected to the memory of his parents and sister, Mrs. Amélie Louise Rives Sigourney (who with her husband perished at sea), were unfortunately destroyed by the burning of the church in 1895. These were also a gift from him, and his watchful care was ever manifested for the preservation and support of this sacred spot. Nor was his liberality confined here, for he entered heartily into every public improvement which would advance and beautify this favored section and ameliorate those around him.

Such is a faint sketch of one of the many noble characters who have dwelt among these hills, whose memory will be cherished and remembered with delight by the rising generation. He died in 1890. A beautiful memorial window now adorns the new Grace Church, erected to his memory by his widow.

Cobham Park is still the home of the family, who visit it frequently during the lovely summer season, when its hospitable doors are thrown open and its grand halls are made to echo the happy voices of many visitors from North and South. During the winter months its gentle mistress resides with her son, Dr. W. C. Rives, of New York, or at her old home in Boston, Massachusetts. Then lovely Cobham Park sits silent, and, like some old English castle, seems to speak in tones of sadness of departed days, when its illustrious head gave it a charm and an attraction such as is rarely possessed by a Virginia home.

THE MACHUNK FARMS

THE CREEK—CAMPBELLS—MACHUNK

THERE are three old homesteads situated along the Machunk Creek standing in all their originality of more than a hundred years ago. These are The Creek farm, the home of Howell Lewis; Campbells, the home of the late Joseph W. Campbell; and Machunk, the home of the Gilmers. It is to be doubted if in any other section there can be found three more antique and interesting buildings than these now standing. Each of them face the Machunk Creek, which runs parallel with the South-West Mountains, and fed by many streams which spring from its mountain-sides, causing the creek at times to assume the proportions of a river. This famous stream, red with Albemarle soil, was named by the Indians "Mauchunk," similar to the mountains of that name in Pennsylvania; but the legend is still told that the name was derived from an Irishman who was crossing the creek on a log, holding in one hand a chunk of fire, which unfortunately he dropped in the deep stream, whereupon he cried out, "Oh, my chunk! my chunk!" from which circumstance the creek was named; but the name has always been written by the earliest inhabitants along its bank "*Machunk*." It starts not far below Cobham Station on the Chesapeake and Ohio Railroad and courses in a south-west direction through a fertile and beautiful valley, which borders the foot-hills of the mountain range, which rise about three miles distant.

The first of these, The Creek farm, has already been mentioned in our description of Music Hall, of which it forms a part. The old building, as has been stated, was the first house of Colonel John Walker, of Belvoir, and was moved from there to Milton by the Hon. Francis Walker, the father of Mrs. William C. Rives, of Castle Hill, who once lived there. After this it was again moved to its present site on the Music Hall tract by Thomas Walker Lewis, who first lived there when he was married; afterwards he moved to Lego, near Pantops.

When Captain Terrell, of Music Hall, died this place was given to his adopted niece, Sarah Stanford, who came to Virginia when quite a child and lived at Music Hall until her marriage with Howell Lewis, when they went to live at The Creek, where they raised a large and interesting family.

The old building still stands clothed in its original rough boards, and presenting much the appearance of the first Clover Fields house, a cut of which has been given. The front is sheltered by a long low porch, from the eaves of which rises a steep roof, dotted with dormer-windows. Each timber, brick, and nail speaks in silent words of a once happy period, and its well-worn floors show where many generations have trod.

SOUTH-WEST MOUNTAINS

The next farm to this, half-way between Cobham and Keswick, and setting about half a mile from the Machunk Creek, is the Campbell mansion. This old building forms a very antique and pretty picture as seen from the distant railroad. Its date of building is possibly anterior to the Creek house, but it presents even a better state of preservation. The putting on a new roof is the only improvement made to the old building for a century. Its original shape and appearance is still unchanged, as when seen by the writer fifty years ago, with its lofty roof, towering chimneys, queer-shaped rooms, and narrow stairway. This is perhaps the best preserved of the old Colonial type of buildings in this neighborhood, and should be preserved in picture and song for future generations.

When this house was built or by whom erected is not known. More than sixty years ago Mr. Joseph W. Campbell, who had married Sarah Rogers, the sister of Lewis Rogers, of Paris, France (who gave the land to his sister), came here to live. Most of this large body of land stretching along the Machunk Creek was an original growth of the finest timber. When, in 1848, the building of the great Chesapeake and Ohio Railroad was first begun at Gordonsville towards the Ohio River, Mr. Campbell obtained the contract for furnishing all the timber required. For this purpose he bought and located the first steam saw-mill in the county, which was placed near the creek, where the railroad was to be built. It was in those days of the old strap-rail, which required long stringers of timber to nail it upon, besides cross-ties which were to be mortised. It can be seen, therefore, the vast quantities of timber required. Besides these, he also furnished the timbers for its many bridges and depot buildings, and did also a large shipping business after the road was completed. As most of the mill-work was done by his many slaves, and being at little expense, Mr. Campbell amassed quite a fortune.

In 1848, Mr. Campbell was contractor for hauling all the stone from the quarries at Peachylorum, near Castle Hill, for the building of Grace Church; but the quantity of stone required was so far beyond his expectations that he lost money upon the venture; not being reimbursed for the extra work, he never entered the new church which his hands had helped to rear. He also opened large lime-quarries on his lands, which proved quite profitable, and largely beneficial to the agriculturist community. Mr. Campbell was very active and industrious in all of his pursuits, though being very fleshy, weighing nearly three hundred pounds; indeed, he would say, with a merry twinkle, that the railroad would have to charge his fare by the ton. Notwithstanding his great bulk, he was an excellent rider, very fond of fox-hunting, and would keep the lead with the youngsters. He was always jolly, of a merry disposition, fond of all sports, especially of fishing, and lived most bountifully in the luxuries of life. His house would be frequently filled with such illus-

SOUTH-WEST MOUNTAINS

trious men as Colonel Fontaine, the president of the Virginia Central Railroad, Lewis Rogers, the millionaire, of Paris, Hon. William C. Rives, the Walkers, and principal men of his day, who knew his worth. His son, William Campbell, succeeded him for a while in the mill business, afterwards going West, where he died unmarried. His son-in-law, S. F. Sampson, lived at the old farm for many years. One daughter, Miss Susan Campbell, still survives and lives at the old homestead, which is now worked by his grandson, Joseph W. Sampson, who recently married Miss Shackleford, of Stony Point, Virginia.

Mr. and Mrs. Campbell both died the same day, and were buried together in the little graveyard near their house.

The Machunk farm comes next in point of interest; indeed, it stands in point of age and historic memories above any of its compeers along the creek. Sitting on a high hill at the head of the Machunk valley, at a point where the railroad sweeps to the west and the creek to the south, it commands one of the most glorious prospects of mountain, valley, and stream that are vouchsafed to any of the many homes in this section.

This old place was first settled and owned by the Gilmers, a family whose celebrity for its eminent men stands forth in brilliant colors on the pages of Virginia's history.

It took its name at an early date from the creek which winds through the farm, the spot where the incident occurred which we have already narrated is supposed to have been here. At first it was called Gilmerton, after the family, but soon after reverted to its original name, Mauchunk or Machunk. The place was first settled by George Gilmer, son of Dr. George Gilmer, of Penn Park, and grandson of the first Dr. George Gilmer, of Williamsburg, Virginia, who came to Virginia in 1731 and married Mary Peachy Walker, sister of "Dr. Tom" Walker, of Castle Hill. George Gilmer married a Miss Hudson, and had several sons and daughters,—Christopher, John Harmer, Thomas Walker Gilmer, governor of Virginia, Juliet, James, Anne, all of whom were born at Machunk. This George Gilmer had a brother, Francis Walker Gilmer, the first law professor at the University of Virginia, having been selected by Mr. Jefferson for that position; he also lived for a time at Machunk, as records show that he was the last of the Gilmers connected with it, and transferred the place to his friend Dabney Minor, who purchased it about 1830.

This Dabney Minor married Martha Jefferson Terrell, a direct descendant of the Carr, Jefferson, and Terrell stock. She was named for her great-grandmother, Martha Jefferson, sister of President Thomas Jefferson, who had married Dabney Carr, the intimate friend of the President. The father of Martha Terrell was Richard Terrell, of Kentucky, who married Lucy, the daughter of Dabney Carr. Dabney Minor, of Machunk, was the son of James and Mary Minor; his first wife was Eliza Johnson, niece of Hon. William Wirt, the historian. Most of these distinguished connections had been visitors to Machunk, making its old halls to witness gatherings where genius, wit, and humor were displayed, and where, doubtless, many scenes of state-craft were enacted.

Mrs. Martha Minor survived her husband many years. During the first deep grief of her widowhood she named the place Retirement, but again this did not stick to the old farm, and its old name cropped up, and has been retained ever since.

After the death of Mr. and Mrs. Dabney Minor the Machunk farm went to their daughter Lucy, who married Colonel Dabney Trice, of Middlesex County, Virginia. Colonel Trice bought of the heirs that portion of the farm called Grassdale, which was not inherited by his wife. This name, too, was soon dropped and merged into that of Machunk.

Colonel Trice obtained his cognomen in the old militia service. He was a man of great intelligence, a most successful farmer, and highly esteemed for his happy, genial disposition and cultivated powers. Colonel Trice, his wife, and all of their children save two died at Machunk, the surviving ones being Lucy L., who married Mr. John Minor, of Gale Hill, and has recently died, and Dr. Dabney Trice, who moved to the West. The old mansion stands as it first came from the hands of George Gilmer, many years ago. It is a low, one-and-a-half storied house, with porticos in front and rear; its lower rooms being larger than usually found in buildings of that period, but its upper ones are of the same diminutive type, showing the economizing of space. Machunk has always been noted for its fertility, its rich flowers, its fine garden, and its extensive meadows stretching far up and down the creek, which, when on a rampage, would entirely overflow this beautiful valley, giving it the appearance of a wide river, which would carry destruction before it.

The Machunk farm has been frequently the scene of much refined gayety. The literary tastes of Mrs. Trice and her daughters were of the highest type, which gave them delight in entertaining those of similar dispositions. Here the charm of bright classic minds, combined with love of poetry, song, and music, made this delightful home one never to be forgotten.

Machunk farm has since passed entirely out of the Trice family, and is now owned by Mr. Charles S. Bowcock, of Keswick, Virginia, a rising and prominent young farmer.

BROAD OAK
The Residence of Edward C Mead, Esq. Enlarged 1874.

BROAD OAK

THE HOME OF EDWARD C. MEAD, ESQ.

IF the lover of the antique, who delights in old moss-covered buildings, whose every plank, shingle, and nail tells the tale of a past century, when building was done under such difficulties by the early settlers, then the Broad Oak house, when first entered in 1861 by its present proprietor, would have rejoiced the heart, and called forth from a poetic nature a pathetic ode. When or by whom the first little one-storied house, having but two rooms, was built is beyond the knowledge of any one now living. A few feet from its front door stood a giant oak, from which it takes its name; it measures twenty feet in circumference at its base, and spreads a shade over the yard of more than eighty feet in diameter each way; it stretches its giant arms over the little dwelling as if in protection of its peaceful occupants, and has sheltered 'neath its dense foliage many generations. This monarch of the forest has been known to the community for its conspicuous size and beauty since the recollection of the oldest inhabitant, who speak of it as being nearly as large a tree in their youth as now. The indications of its extreme age are now manifest, and this patriarch of the original forest is gradually failing in strength, as shown by its decaying limbs and withering leaves; yet it still forms in its graceful old age a particular and striking object, as being one of the few familiar landmarks of this historic region. Three more oaks, nearly as large, also stand in rear of the house, one of which was struck by lightning in 1888, and immediately died. Stepping into the house, the first object to strike the visitor's notice is its rough floor of wide plank, without tongue or groove, and nailed with large wrought nails from a common forge; its shingles were moss-covered, and put on with similar nails, though smaller; its chimney was half stone and half brick, the latter being much larger in size than the present kind. Its huge framing timbers measured twelve by fourteen inches for the sills, and four by eight for the sleepers and joists, all being hewed by hand, and as sound as when put in. The cellar and foundation walls were of stone, fourteen inches thick, and cemented with mud mortar. The one largest room was sixteen feet square, while the little garret rooms were mere cubby-holes, in which one could scarcely stand erect. Such was the first house at Broad Oak. About 1840 an addition was made by a two-story room joined to this old part, and in 1874 the old part was raised another story to correspond with it, placing all under one roof, as is shown in the engraving. There are other evidences which tend to establish the very early settlement of Broad Oak. Immediately in front of the house (as was the superstitious custom in those days) was the remains of an old graveyard, but without any headstones. A few feet from the front door also showed the site of a well, but tradition says that its waters were so bitter of mineral that it was filled up, under the belief of being a judgment for having been placed so near the graveyard. Since then, however, another well has been opened in rear of the house, and its waters also partake of a strong mineral character, but which have proved to be an excellent tonic. But the strongest proof in evidence of its being settled early in the eighteenth century is that of a Colonial penny which was ploughed up near the dwelling in 1863. This penny has on one side a shield surmounted by a crown, upon which are quartered the arms of England, Ireland, Scotland, and *Virginia*, the whole encircled with the word " Virginia, 1773;" on the reverse side was a head with the words " Georgius III. Rex." This proves the origin of the term " Old Dominion," Virginia being thus acknowledged a part of England in gratitude for her loyalty. There have also been found upon the place many perfect Indian arrow-heads, which have been placed in the Smithsonian Institution at Washington. These evidently show that this once formed the camping-ground of the Indians or marked the site of a battle.

The land upon which Broad Oak is situated was formerly owned by the Rev. John Rogers, of Keswick, and was afterwards hallowed by the presence of the Rev. Dr. Alfred Holliday, who resided here for many years as pastor of the South

Plains Presbyterian Church, which is in full view. After the death of Mr. Rogers the place passed into the hands of his son, John A. Rogers, who, in 1858, sold it to Charles E. Taylor, of Petersburg, Virginia. This gentleman lived but a short while, dying early in 1861. During the few years of his occupancy he made many improvements and added much to the beauty and fertility of the place. After his death it was again sold, and on the 4th of October, 1861, its present owner, while standing under the noble oak at its doorstep, made the highest bid, which placed the property in his hands.

There are few places along the South-West Mountains having a more beautiful landscape spread before its door, from which can be seen the entire range of undulating hills rising in majestic height, with their highest peaks and knobs, like giant citadels, guarding the quiet valley below. On the extreme left stands lofty Monticello, with Carter's Mountain towering above it, and the eye then sweeps the range to Peter's Mountain on the extreme right, which marks the highest elevation, while immediately in front sits the little station of Keswick, where the trains of the Chesapeake and Ohio Railroad pass in view daily, while dotting the foot-hills are seen many of the homesteads here described. The present owner has endeavored to beautify and adorn the surroundings of this old home so favored by nature; its sloping lawn is filled with stately fruit-trees and shrubbery, which glory in radiant colors during the opening spring, while its grand old oaks surrounding the mansion make it most conspicuous from a distance. Thus Broad Oak has always been famous for its fruits and flowers, which have afforded pleasure and delight to the many who have honored it with a visit. To the young it has often been a scene of gayety, its halls resounding with music and the joyful voices of happy hearts, while to the aged the view of " the everlasting hills" and the peaceful calm have been ever a refreshing feast.

It may be pardoned the writer if he speaks of his own family in connection with Broad Oak; at least, he is not ashamed of his ancestry, and can boast of a lineage which may bear the scrutiny of the most exacting " Son of the Revolution." The Mead or Meade family is one of the most widespread and ancient of any in the country, members of it being found in nearly every State of the Union. The English Meades were of the nobility, the family in this country springing from Dr. Richard Mead, who was born at Stepney, England, 1673. He became very distinguished in his profession, and was vice-president of the Royal Society, censor of the College of Physicians, and physician to George II. He interested himself much in the introduction of inoculation for the small-pox, and assisted in the preliminary experiments made upon criminals. He wrote many valuable treatises, among which were " A Mechanical Account of Poisons," " Discourse concerning Pestilential Contagion," " De Imperiis Solis ac Lunæ, in Corpora humana et Morbis inde oriundis," " De Morbis Biblicis," and " Monita Medica." For his valuable services to science he was knighted in 1722. He died in 1754. The Mead(e) family came to this country shortly after the " Mayflower," and first settled at Horseneck (now Greenwich), Connecticut. From this first family of the name located in this country descended General John Mead of the Revolution, who served under Washington, and was distinguished throughout the war for bravery. He died in 1797, his will being witnessed by a Zachariah Mead, one of the family, on the 24th of March of that year. The English way of spelling the name was with a final " e," but this was dropped by General Mead for some reason, though retained by the family in other States. Bishop Meade, of Virginia, who averred that the two families were of the same stock, gives his great-grandfather as of Irish descent, who emigrated to this country, married a Quakeress in Flushing, New York, and settled in Suffolk, Virginia. This may have been some time after the landing of the first Meads in Connecticut, but doubtless were of the same English origin. The coat of arms of the English Meades, as taken from the Heralds' College, England, are thus described: " Sa. cher. erbet s Pel. Vul," with the motto " Semper Paratus," the translation of which is, " Sable Field-chevron," represented as two rafters of a house joined together; the chevron is gold color, but powdered black; three pelicans wounding themselves, according to the old tradition that the pelican picked its own breast to nourish its young. The symbol of the pelican is Generation, Preservation, Education, and Good Example. The motto signifies "Always Ready," which has been strikingly exemplified by many of the family. It is singular to remark that though originally of the Roman Church on one side, intermixed with the Quaker and Unitarian faith on the other, yet with scarcely an exception the family have strictly adhered to the Protestant Episcopal Church in America, many of whom have become prominent, especially those of the Virginia branch, represented by Bishop Meade, his sons and grandsons, while the descendants of the Connecticut Meads were represented in the Virginia Diocese quite early in the person of Rev. Zachariah Mead, and now by his grandson, Rev. George Otis Mead, of Casanova, Fauquier County, Virginia. On his maternal side, Mr. E. C. Mead is great-grandson of General William Hull of the Revolutionary war and that of 1812; a biography of his military and civil life was written by his grandson, the late Dr. James Freeman Clarke, of Boston, Massachusetts.

Mr. Edward C. Mead married, November 21, 1861, Emily Augusta Burgoyne, eldest daughter of H. A. Burgoyne, Esq., formerly of New York, and now of Maryland. He was son of the late William Burgoyne, who lived for many years at Charleston, South Carolina, after which he moved to New York City, there amassing a large fortune by investments in city real estate during its rapid expansion. Mrs. Mead is also closely connected with the Mosers of Philadelphia represented by the

HISTORIC HOMES

late Dr. Philip Moser; also with the Haights, Lawrences, and Rosseters, of New York, and through the latter family reaching back to Benjamin Franklin. Her grandmother, Mrs. Edward J. Rosseter, while living in Bridgeport, Connecticut, about 1830, had a slave of the Franklin family as a servant in her household. The children of Mr. and Mrs. E. C. Mead are:

1. Henry Burgoyne Mead, now of Chicago, Illinois.
2. William Zachariah Mead, of Richmond, Virginia; married, June 24, 1889, Myra Fisk Hilton, of Chicago, Illinois. Their children are: Bertha Blanchard and Emily Burgoyne.
3. Frances Meriwether Mead; married, September 3, 1896, Francis R. Hewitt, of North Carolina.
4. Edward Augustus Mead; died June 11, 1874.
5. Rev. George Otis Mead; married, November 24, 1897, Lilian Minty, of Chicago, Illinois. She died September 22, 1898, leaving one son, Lynne Burgoyne.
6. Mary Rossiter Mead.
7. Annie Louisa Mead.
8. Ernest Campbell Mead.

KESWICK STATION

CHESAPEAKE AND OHIO RAILROAD

MORE particular mention should be made of this the central point of the South-West Mountain region, historic as being as far east as Sheridan reached in his memorable raid into Albemarle in 1865, leaving the place in ashes, being one of the last sad scenes of the closing war.

In 1849, when the Virginia Central Railroad reached this point in its stretch for the Ohio River, it was undecided whether to have the "depot," as the stations were then called, here, at Edgehill, or at Shadwell, the birthplace of Jefferson. Colonel T. J. Randolph was solicitous to have it at his farm, Edgehill, but the majority of the farmers along its line prevailed in having two established,—one at the Keswick farm, where it intersects the county road, the other at Shadwell Mills, upon the river. For a long time the "Keswick Depot" was but a small affair, being scarcely more than a "turnout" or switch station, having one or two small buildings. Shadwell was then the great emporium for this section, being quite a town; but the failure to rebuild its large carding-factory caused its rapid decline, and in recent years it has ceased to be even a "depot," which has been removed to Edgehill, the spot at first contemplated by "Colonel

Jeff" Randolph, but which still retains the name of Shadwell, in honor of Jefferson's birthplace. After the decline of "Shadwell Depot," Keswick arose in magnitude and importance. At an early date, even before the advent of the railroad, there was near the place a grist- and saw-mill, and not far off the Presbyterian South Plains Church, and it soon began to assume the proportions of a village; but the capture of the place by Sheridan, and burning of the mill, depot building, and warehouse, completely wiped out the little place for a time. Among the incidents of this exciting event was one which proved the faithfulness of the old negro miller.

The mill was in charge of one of the slaves of the Rogers farm, who held the keys with domineering sway over its management, and it is said even his old mistress would have to beg for meal. When he heard that the "Yankees" were coming, he hid the keys and also several bags of meal. When the troops demanded entrance, "Old Ned" positively refused, whereupon he was threatened with violence, but intimidation had no effect, and with folded arms he watched the destruction of his favorite mill. After the departure of the troops he carried to his old mistress the few bags of meal, saying, "Dey didn't git de las' grinding, nohow."

In recent years Keswick has risen to a place of some importance. It now contains a large brick depot and reception-room, three stores, with several shops, drug-store, express, mail, and telegraph

SOUTH-WEST MOUNTAINS

station, and telephone connection with Charlottesville and other points. Several handsome residences are also scattered around its suburbs, forming quite a picturesque and busy place.

It is here that the railroad makes a sudden bend from the east. Sweeping through the lower woodlands, it aims straight for the mountains, a mile distant, and as the train emerges from the forest the full view of Keswick, with the South-West range, breaks upon the delighted vision of the traveller.

Colonel H. W. Fuller, general passenger agent of the road, has been quite partial to Keswick and this beautiful section of his road, placing here all the modern improvements of a first-class station for the benefit of the neighborhood. During the summer months Keswick becomes the daily rendezvous for the many visitors who seek this healthy region, making it one of excitement and bustle as each train unloads its quota of happy young people; here the *beau monde* of the heated cities seeks to expand its lungs and stretch its limbs over the rugged mountain slopes; here the gayeties of fashionable resorts are to be met with in a modified form, the many homesteads along the hills resounding with music and the dance; here, too, the more exciting music of the hounds is frequently heard along the mountain-sides, urging the young Nimrod to the chase; and more recently a handsome club hall has here been erected, where the ambitious tyro of the stage can strut its boards in mimic play, or amateurs can warble

HISTORIC HOMES

sweet notes upon the moonlit air in melodious concert. Such are a few of the attractions of which Keswick Station is the centre, and for which it has already attained a great celebrity, such as will increase each year as it becomes more widely known.

Mr. P. B. Hancock, its present very able and efficient agent, has retained his position since 1874, winning the confidence and esteem of his superior officers and of the travelling public, who will here be cordially met by him and directed to the many points of interest along these beautiful mountains.

EVERETTSVILLE

NOW LA FOURCHE, THE HOME OF THE BOWCOCKS.

WE cannot pass this once noted place without a hasty glance, as it forms one of the truly historic landmarks along the South-West Mountains.

The place derives its name from the elder Dr. Charles Everett, of Belmont, upon whose lands it was situated. It is located in the fork of the county road from Charlottesville, one branch of which turns to the south, leading to Richmond by the old "Three Notch" road, one of the first to be opened by the early settlers; the other branch turns to the north-east, leading to Gordonsville and Washington. On both of these roads the travel was very great before the age of steam. All the products of this region passed over them, as well as the large passenger travel by stages. It was early in the present century quite an important place, having a tavern, store, shops, and stables for the exchange of stage horses. Here was also the post-office for this region, and was the precinct for elections, when the honest mode of voting *viva voce* prevailed; this, too, was the rendezvous for the sturdy farmers on muster days, when the youthful patriots would be enthused with military ambition.

Here, too, would be the stopping-place for those old-time shows on wheels, which would pitch their tents, to the delight of black and white, for a large circuit.

The old tavern, which was standing even to 1860 in quite good preservation, had sheltered many of the most noted men of the past, some of whom were distinguished foreigners on their way to visit Monticello, which is here in full view. It is said that at this point General Lafayette met the cavalcade sent from Charlottesville to receive him when last on his visit to this country, and when he alighted and beheld Monticello in the distance he took off his hat in salutation of its distinguished occupant, who was there waiting to receive him with open arms.

This, too, was the spot where, in 1863, "Stonewall" Jackson with his army corps rested in the grove of woods which surrounds Everettsville while on his forced march from the Valley of Virginia to the defence of Richmond; here, underneath these shady oaks, the great chieftain laid with his weary men, while the original old "Stonewall" band filled the woods with the stirring strains of "Dixie."

Everettsville continued to be the central point of attraction up to the year 1849, when the establishment of Keswick Station took its glory away, and the good old stage days ceased.

In 1860 Everettsville was purchased by Dr. Charles S. Bowcock, son of the late Colonel J. J. Bowcock, who for many years was presiding justice for the county of Albemarle. Dr. Bowcock

SOUTH-WEST MOUNTAINS

married the same year he bought the place Miss Margaret Branch, daughter of William Mosely Branch, of Goochland County, Virginia. The family of Bowcock is quite an ancient one. It was originally spelled *Beaucoke*, a man of this name having come from Scotland to America during the last century, his sons settling in different parts of the country, but soon the name changed to *Bowcock*. The joke goes between the Hon. Thos. S. Bocock and Colonel J. J. Bowcock, who were cousins, that Thomas often laughed at the colonel saying that he had put that " w" in his name because he was such a *Whig*, and the colonel retorted by saying that Thomas was such a *Democrat* that he had dropped out the " w" entirely.

Dr. Bowcock died in 1895, after serving the community for more than thirty years as its physician.

The children of Dr. and Mrs. Bowcock are:

1. William Branch Bowcock; died in 1884 just after having graduated in medicine.
2. Robert Lee Bowcock; married, in 1889, Virginia Sands, daughter of Alexander H. Sands, a prominent lawyer of Richmond, Virginia. Dr. R. Lee Bowcock is now a practising physician of Anniston, Alabama.
3. Mary Stewart Bowcock; married, in 1891, Conway Robinson Sands, Commonwealth's attorney in Richmond, Virginia.
4. Charles S. Bowcock; married Miss Anna Gaines Early in 1897.

Soon after taking possession of Everettsville, Dr. Bowcock entirely remodelled the old tavern and re-

HISTORIC HOMES

moved all the surrounding buildings. The mansion now presents quite a tasty and commodious country-seat, surrounded by a grove of stately trees and ornamental plants, which is in marked contrast to the old tavern, with its tap-room, wash-room, and small bedrooms, of the stage-coach era.

GLENMORE

THE HOME OF THE MAGRUDERS

GLENMORE presents the appearance of one of those old English manors during the early years of the present century. It sits upon a high ridge of hills, flanked on each side by tangled glens of original growth, hence its name. From its lofty windows, which peer above the tree-tops, can be viewed Monticello and the full range of the mountains, not far distant, while to the south-west stretch the fertile plains of the Rivanna River, which courses along the greater portion of the farm. While the mansion has a baronial, antique aspect, with its lofty pillars, long double porticos, and tall windows, from floor to ceiling, it is evidently of a more advanced order of architecture, and does not come under the Colonial type. The first house to be built stands in its rear. The exact date of its construction is not known, but supposed to be about 1800.

The first to live at Glenmore was Thomas Mann Randolph, Jr., the son of Thomas Mann Randolph, of Edgehill, whose second wife, Gabriella Harvie, of Belmont, must have inherited this portion of old Harvie's estate, upon which her son resided for a time. He was succeeded in the ownership by a Watkins. After this it was rented to the father of the late Dr. Howard, of Buckeyeland, Virginia.

The house tract was one moiety of the Watkins estate, which was bought by the late Colonel B. H. Magruder to be added to his wife's portion, which comprised nine hundred and sixty acres of the Minor tract, by original grant from King George in 1732, and came into the Minor family, through Martin Dawson, in 1800.

Colonel B. H. Magruder was born in 1812, the son of Rev. J. B. Magruder, an eminent preacher in the Methodist Church, who owned many thousand acres of land, stretching from Boyd Tavern, south-east, for a good distance along the Rivanna River, which embraced some of its richest bottom-lands. Boyd was his son-in-law, and got the tavern, which has always retained his name. He first opened the tavern and a store there, which after his death were continued by his widow, and have since passed into several hands.

Colonel Magruder came into possession of his father's large estate and settled at Glenmore about 1832. Colonel Benjamin H. Magruder was among the first law graduates of the University of Virginia. He was an officer in the Virginia State Militia force, but was too old to enter the last war. He took a prominent stand at the bar quite early, and, entering politics, was sent to the Virginia Legislature in 1850, where he continued to represent his county each session until 1870. As a speaker he stood foremost among his political contemporaries, and by his eloquence and deep interest in

SOUTH-WEST MOUNTAINS

his county's welfare became very popular and won the high esteem and confidence of his countrymen. As a man of deep learning, a sound thinker, and a great lover of the poetical and beautiful in literature, none who enjoyed his society could fail to be impressed.

Colonel Magruder married first a Miss Minor, by whom were six children:

1. John Bankhead Magruder, M.A. of the University of Virginia; was colonel of the Fifty-Seventh Virginia Infantry, Armistead's Brigade, C. S. A. He fell upon the bloody field of Gettysburg, *inside* of the enemy's works, during the fearful charge of Pickett's division, which was enfiladed by a heavy fire of grapeshot.
2. Henry M. Magruder; graduated in law at the University of Virginia; held an appointment under the United States government at Blacksburg College, Virginia, and also several county offices; died in 1885.
3. Horatio E. Magruder, a most successful farmer; resides on the homestead at Glenmore; married Mrs. Julia Wallace, *née* Chewning, of Milton, Albemarle County, Virginia.
4. Julia; married Mr. Tyler, of Caroline County, Virginia, member of the Legislature of Virginia.
5. Evelyn; married Mr. De Jarnette, of Spottsylvania County, Virginia, a member of the Virginia Legislature.
6. Sally; married Colonel Stewart, of Portsmouth, Virginia, a prominent lawyer.

Colonel Magruder married second Miss Eveline Norris, sister of the late Dr. Norris, of Charlottesville, Virginia, by whom were four children:

HISTORIC HOMES OF THE

1. Dr. Edward May Magruder, a prominent physician, of Charlottesville, Virginia; married Miss Mary Cole Gregory, of King William County, Virginia, December 16, 1896.
2. Opie E. Magruder, civil engineer, of Winston, North Carolina.
3. George Mason Magruder, surgeon in the United States Marine Hospital service, Galveston, Texas; married, January 6, 1896, Miss Isadora Carvallo Causton, of Washington, D.C.
4. Edgar W. Magruder, professor of chemistry in Johns Hopkins University, Baltimore, Maryland.

The Glenmore mansion has always been most attractive, not only to the eminent and gifted in public positions but to the young people, whom the colonel was particularly fond of having around him. At these gay assemblages he would always attract their young minds by his own love of poetry and literature, and by his wonderful conversational powers would charm them with his beautiful imagery and thought, until their ambition would be fired with zealous emulation, which many who have since attained distinction owe to his kind and solicitous influence.

With Glenmore, the home of patriotism, learning, and culture, which sits near to Monticello, from where we started on the tour of the South-West Mountain homes, we close the series, having made the circuit of the range to the north-east and back.

It is most fitting here to end them for this, the east, side of the mountains. Jefferson, the father of Democracy, starting the country on its suc-

SOUTH-WEST MOUNTAINS

cessful career, which was not broken until 1861, and Magruder, who stood in the legislative halls during that terrible strife, saw the end of his once proud State as it fell by overwhelming numbers of a sectional party; but, like Marmion of old, he rallied his State to industrial efforts of recuperation, and lived to see her once more upon a career of prosperity.

THE END

www.ingramcontent.com/pod-product-compliance
Lightning Source LLC
Chambersburg PA
CBHW030802230426
43667CB00008B/1030